FIRST DAYS OF MARRIAGE

TO: Lavern + Mark

9-20-96

From: Maude Lyons
+ Family

May you have a blessed
marriage.

First Days of Marriage

DEVOTIONS TO HELP THE TWO OF YOU BECOME ONE

Mary Harwell Sayler

BROADMAN & HOLMAN PUBLISHERS

Nashville, Tennessee

4253–82
0–8054–5382–2

Dewey Decimal Classification: 242.644
Subject Heading: Devotional Literature \ Marriage
Library of Congress Card Catalog Number: 94–44032

Library of Congress Cataloging-in-Publication Data

Sayler, Mary Harwell.
First days of marriage : devotions to help the two of you become one / Mary Harwell Sayler.
p. cm.
ISBN 0–8054–5382–2
1. Married people—Prayer-books and devotions—English. 2. Young adults—Prayer-books and devotions—English. 3. Devotional calendars. I. Title.
BV4529.2.S28 1995
242'.644—dc20 94–44032
CIP

This book is, of course, dedicated to my husband, friend, lover, companion, family leader, business manager, practical advice-giver, handyman, woodworker, dishwasher, Bible study and manuscript assistant, and life partner in prayer, Robert Henry Sayler.

Bob and I married May 11, 1962, in Seattle, Washington, his hometown. I'd left Florida to stay with my sister in Fort Lewis, Washington. So Bob's and my "home" became anywhere between the northwest and southeast corners of the United States. After his army days ended, airline days began. We moved around the country toward many changes and challenges, but always seeking and finding a church home.

At first, we didn't know to look for the Lord's help in daily matters. Yet, from the start, God drew us to read the Bible together every night. Later we added prayers, then realized we could pray anytime —even *during* an argument!

Once sought, God put to work His word and timing and the counsel of pastors to lead Bob into his own financial planning business in DeLand, Florida—our home since 1981. Having always stayed home to be with our children and write, I began to concentrate on Bible study and teaching what I'd learned about the written word. And Bob, well, he became the only stockbroker I know who prays with clients.

We've seen so many changes and surprises, we know God has more to come. Every night, we still read the Bible and pray. And we still get amazed at the way God brings together His people, plans, and purpose. But nothing seems more astonishing than seeing the Lord take two such different individuals and make them one in Him.

Introduction

Something wonderful has happened! You've fallen—or perhaps floated—into love. You've made a commitment to each other that goes far beyond just seeing how things "work out." You've decided to devote your lives to one another in the Lord.

In these very first days of marriage, you begin a unique, lasting relationship—a marriage devoted to God. So find out what He has to say. From the start, seek Him in prayer, Bible study, and daily devotion to His word. Listen to Him and each other. Let Him build your individual faith in Jesus Christ, the cornerstone of your married life. Let God's word strengthen your respect, trust, and love as you commit yourselves and your marriage to Him, forever.

Whether you know the Bible exceptionally well, very little, or not at all, you will *always* have more to learn. To start, find a translation of the Bible you especially like. You have many excellent choices, but in these pages you will find Scriptures from the following versions:

AMP = Scripture taken from *The Amplified Bible*, Old Testament copyright © 1965, 1987 by the Zondervan Corporation. The Amplified New Testament copyright © 1958, 1987 by the Lockman Foundation. Used by permission.

KJV = *King James Version*—English translation of ancient texts authorized by King James of England.

NIV = Scripture taken from the *Holy Bible, New International Version,* copyright © 1973, 1978, 1984, International Bible Society. Used by permission of Zondervan Bible Publishers.

NRSV = *New Revised Standard Version Bible,* copyright © 1989 by the Division of Christian Education of the National Council of the Churches of Christ in the United States of America.

This is the day which
the Lord hath made;
we will rejoice and be glad in it.
(Psalm 118:24, KJV)

Congratulations! You've dreamed about this day all of your life—or at least this past week. Now it's here: Your wedding day! You're so excited, you can hardly wait another moment. But be honest. Haven't you thought about hopping a train to Bermuda and drowning along the way?

Wet feet can't be encouraged on this electric occasion, but you can expect *cold* feet. So consider: How cold are you—cold as in dead, passionless, icy, or frozen? Or do you feel cold as in suddenly coming down with a case of sniffles, shivers, or feverish activity?

No matter how much two people love each other, they'll often feel like weeping, hiding, and/or running away as the wedding date draws near. That's perfectly normal—as in *to be expected.* But if you truly cannot rejoice in this day—if you're not the least bit glad in it—don't get out of the predicament by train. Fly!

Before you can say, "I do," and mean it, you need to be able to say, "I don't!" Even with the wedding march playing, it is not too late to realize, "I don't want to marry this person—ever." More likely though, your cold feet will warm as you remember, "I don't want to be without the one I love."

If the One you love is Christ Jesus, you've prayed for Him to show you the person you're to marry. You've followed His lead into this relationship. And with Him, you've waited for this day to arrive—your wedding day, which the Lord hath made. So rejoice and be glad in it as you keep this date with Him.

Prayer: Heavenly Father, I'm scared. Help me to remember that You're my first love. And Lord, please speak now and forever hold my peace in Jesus' name.

Journey with God: So why do you want to get married? Make a date with each other to discuss this with God. In the space below, write down what comes to you—thoughts and feelings you'll want to remember throughout your married life.

Therefore a man leaves his father and his mother and clings to his wife, and they become one flesh.
(Genesis 2:24, NRSV)

"Who presents this woman and this man to be married to one another?"

In a traditional wedding ceremony, the bride's father, stepfather, grandfather, or perhaps uncle "gives her away." Since the groom presumably takes her, some might assume this makes the bride his property. But the real giveaway is the family's permission to marry.

According to tradition, the man doesn't need parental consent. But, according to God's word, he must now separate himself from his father and mother, so the end result is the same: The bride leaves her family, the groom leaves his, and together they become another family—husband and wife.

As you exchange vows, a household that never before existed suddenly comes into being. Pronouncement of you as "husband and wife" actually announces the birth of a brand-new home. You're now kindred, a clan, another notch on the family tree.

Eventually, you might expand to be a father, mother, and child, but size won't change what you've just become. Whether you're two people or ten, your immediate family immediately consists of members who love each other, respect and honor each other, remain faithful to each other, and stay with each other no matter how rich, poor, sick, or well each other gets.

That's how it is in families. People take care of each other—and care about each other too. But before you create this bond in marriage, you first separate yourself from those who raised you and become united in the holy wedlock of your one new family.

Prayer: Heavenly Father, thank You for bringing us together in You. Please help us to have and to hold each other from this day forward in Christ's name.

Journey with God: Ask God how He wants you to "leave" your parents: physically, mentally, emotionally, and financially. Prayerfully listen to the thoughts He brings to your mind.

Neither is there salvation in any other: for there is none other name under heaven given among men, whereby we must be saved.
(Acts 4:12, KJV)

"With this ring I thee wed." What a wonderful moment. As you speak each other's name and slip the rings onto your fingers, you give yourselves to one another to have and to hold. From this day forward, your rings symbolize your vow—your agreement to care about one another—forever.

Even before you finalized your marriage vows, you had already begun to make promises to each other. For instance, when you first decided to get married, you may have promised to find a certain type of ring. Maybe you pledged yourselves to a rental agreement or a mortgage on your first house. And before the wedding, you implied your promise to show up!

Promises. Promises. Throughout your married life you'll do well to make them sparingly since the more you promise, the more you have to keep. You've given your word, right? Well, on your wedding invitations, marriage license, and in the ceremony you've also given each other your good name.

God gave His promise in the name of Jesus. He gave His word. In Him you have the only real hope, the only real promise of a blessed life together. With or without a fancy setting, God's word in Christ fits you as snugly as a ring.

Rich or poor, Christ's saving love surrounds you. Sick or healthy, Christ's saving love surrounds you. In life or in death, Christ's saving love surrounds you. Let the familiar ring of this all-encompassing truth surround you with endless blessing. From this day forward, make yourselves a promise to have and to hold God's pledge to you in Jesus' name.

Prayer: Heavenly Father, help us to love and to cherish each other—and You—always. Help us to keep our word. Thank You for Your vow to us in the word and name of Jesus.

Journey with God: You've probably decided if you'll share one last name, but have you discussed the One name that lasts? Talk with God and each other about your personal vows to Him.

Great is the mystery of godliness:
God was manifest in the flesh,
justified in the Spirit,
seen of angels,
preached unto the Gentiles,
believed on in the world,
received up into glory.
(1 Timothy 3:16b, KJV)

Did you have the blessing of a church wedding? If so, you probably enjoyed a reception afterward. Or perhaps a parent, sibling, or friend invited everyone for an informal gathering in your honor.

Casual or black-tie, large or small, any reception makes the bride and groom the center of attention. People embrace you, congratulate you, kiss you, and thump your back. Some may give a word or two of advice. Others may force themselves to be polite, but *everyone* notices you.

Meanwhile, flashing cameras capture the glorious scene—not necessarily as you see yourselves, but as others see you.

"Oh, what a beautiful bride!"

"And doesn't the groom look handsome?"

Even if you woke up with hives and baggy eyes, your happiness shows. A joyful, loving spirit prevails on this wondrous occasion, so people who aren't fond of you have the grace to keep quiet as others proclaim you "a good-looking couple." You are good-looking too. Justified by the Holy Spirit of Christ's love, no one could possibly be more beautiful, more handsome, or more attractive to God.

Just as you graciously receive guests at the wedding reception, Christ graciously receives you. He presents you, pure and blameless, to the Heavenly Father—not in your own glory, but in His. From your first day of marriage, you can come together receiving God with the radiance of Christ's forgiving love.

Prayer: Holy Father, thank You for Your reception of us into Your kingdom in Jesus' name.

Journey with God: Isn't it glorious? At Christ's invitation, the Almighty God welcomes you. Think about this. Talk about this with each other and with God.

So they are no longer two, but one flesh. Therefore what God has joined together, let no one separate.
(Matthew 19:6, NRSV)

Before you said, "I do," you knew what you were getting into, right? You made a commitment to each other, yes, but what's the big deal? You've been committed before.

Over the years you've made commitments to doing as well as you can in your home, church, community, work, or school. You have already taken on duties, responsibilities, obligations, accountability, contractual agreements, and/or other promises of trying to do a decent job—whether you feel like it at the time or not!

If you put all of those commitments into one legally binding contract, you might catch a glimpse of the hard work you've gotten yourself into. But you won't begin to see the joy. Although you may have already discovered the joys of sex, that's not all you've gotten yourself into either!

In these first days of marriage, you're somewhat like a kid starting school. You know that one plus one makes two. Then suddenly you discover it doesn't. You learn that marriage is neither a plus nor a minus. It's a *times.*

When you exchanged wedding vows, you became two people—united in holy wedlock—as one. Your sexual union embraces that truth. Your union with God binds it securely. In Him, you don't become one person *plus* another job or another duty or another commitment. You become one person *times* another: 1 x 1 = 1.

So one person times one person equals one person. It's not judgmental nor even just mathematical. Your marriage commitment is a spiritual and emotional fact: No one can separate one without dividing one in two. As anyone who's undergone a divorce can tell you, that's a *very* big deal.

Prayer: Oh, Lord, let nothing separate us from each other or the love of Christ.

Journey with God: Did your parents or anyone close to you get divorced? Pray for health for each divided person. Ask God about His times multiplied in you as you become one with Him.

And the man and his wife were both naked, and were not embarrassed or ashamed in each other's presence.
(Genesis 2:25, AMP)

Unless you grew up in a very cold, very remote region, you've probably seen how the human body looks. The physical differences between the opposite sex comes as no big surprise to you. However, with the intrusion of nudity in television, movies, and magazines, something shameful happened. Instead of becoming free to accept one's own sexuality, people began to compare.

"Wow! I wish I had her figure."

"Yeah, I wish you did too."

Or, "Man, what a hunk!"

"So? What does that make me—fat?"

If you came to marriage with mental or physical pictures of how you want yourself and your spouse to look, get rid of them right away. Photographs and fantasies will not help you accept your own body, much less your partner's.

Comparing yourselves with current "sex symbols" leaves you feeling ashamed of how you look and also embarrassed by imperfections in your spouse. You do have some flaws, right? Yet something about you and your mate attracted each other, so whatever it is, hey, enjoy it!

God didn't make any human body for you to covet, lust after, copy, or compare. He made you to be the person you are and to enjoy another's sexual company. So turn out the lights if you like, but don't turn off the spark between you by letting each other's size, shape, or appearance dim beside someone else. You've nothing to be ashamed of. So it'd be a *real shame* to compare yourselves.

Prayer: Heavenly Father, thank You for creating us exactly as You did. Thank You for giving us pleasure in each other's company. Help us to accept our bodily imperfections, not as flaws or something to compare, but as a unique part of Your perfect design for us in Jesus' name.

Journey with God: What features do you most like or enjoy about yourself and your marriage partner? Discuss these with each other and with God. (Don't worry. He won't be shocked.)

Shun immorality and all sexual looseness [flee from impurity in thought, word, or deed.] Any other sin which a man commits is one outside the body, but he who commits sexual immorality sins against his own body.
(1 Corinthians 6:18, AMP)

"And forsaking all others, be faithful as long as you both shall live."

Part of your wedding vows included your promise to be faithful to one another. But in these very first days of marriage you might have broken faith without even knowing. For example, if you've been lustily recalling a former sexual partner, you have not yet "forsaken all others."

Unlike sexual experimentation, marriage ties cannot be treated loosely. They must be secured well with trust or they won't hold you together very long. But before you can "tie the knot" of faithfulness with your spouse, you need to rid yourself of any loose bonds still entwining you to the past. This includes any sexual looseness you had prior to marriage—in reality but also in thought.

To find freedom from premarital unions, including those fantasies, don't trouble your mate, but do talk to God about them. Confession allows you to repent—that is, turn away from or shun sexual looseness or immorality—in each area of your body, heart, and mind. Just by making up your mind to forsake all others, your body and heart will follow your decision—and your spouse—faithfully.

God created marriage. He ordained your union when you exchanged vows. So as you decide to obey Him, trust Him to secure His vow in you. "Tie the knot" of a strong marriage with God's promise not to forsake you. He gives His word for longer than you both shall live.

Prayer: Holy Father, thank You for bringing us together in Your word and ours. Help us to accept Your forgiveness and shun the very thought of past encounters. Help us to forsake all others but You in Jesus' name.

Journey with God: In private, talk with God about your sexual memories, real or imagined. Confess any acts of immorality in word, thought, or deed. Then use this space to write a prayer for the strength and faithfulness of your marriage union.

The husband should give to his wife her conjugal rights (goodwill, kindness, and what is due her as his wife), and likewise the wife to her husband.
(1 Corinthians 7:3, AMP)

Did you "save" yourself for marriage? If so, that's a wonderful gift. Not only did you present your own priceless body to your partner in marriage, but you've brought a unique unopened treasure, waiting to be found.

Without sexual experience, you might feel nervous, fearful, unsure of yourself, or shy. That's to be expected in these first days of marriage as you get to know each other more intimately. Male or female, you might even wonder what to do. For both of you, the answer is—in love and in like—respond.

As you bring yourself to this marriage union, you place yourself into your spouse's hands. Your partner also gives him- or herself to you, but not to do with as you please. Instead, you please each other as you treat each other's body with the utmost kindness and goodwill.

Good will come from this! "Good" sex and good pleasure will come in good time. So don't rush your lovemaking even if it seems long overdue. Give each other the love that's promised by enjoyably concentrating, not on yourself or your own needs, but on those of your marriage partner.

At first you won't know what pleases you, much less your mate. So you just might have to ask. Although it's not the optimum time for a lengthy discussion, it is time for a passionate response to what you like. You owe that loving answer to your spouse. As you give each other what's due, your debt of love will forever be outstanding.

Prayer: Dear God, thank You for the passion of lovemaking! Help us to respond to one another and to You in Jesus' name.

Journey with God: Do you have any sexual concerns? Ask God to bring to your mind whatever inhibits you from responding as you or your partner would like.

Day 9

For the wife does not have [exclusive] authority and control over her own body, but the husband [has his rights]; likewise also the husband does not have [exclusive] authority and control over his body, but the wife [has her rights].
(1 Corinthians 7:4, AMP)

Have you wondered how much sex is too much—or too little? In this well-informed society, you can probably find all sorts of statistics on the subject, but they really don't have anything to do with you. The timing that suits you and your spouse is *your* answer—no one else's.

For most newlyweds, a honeymoon allows an opportunity to discover more about each other. Away from jobs or school, couples relax in the highly romantic atmosphere and feel less awkward in the intimate company marriage brings. But even if they must get back to a routine the very next morning, most newlywed couples find the energy to enjoy conjugal rights.

Problems can occur, though, if one partner shows more energy than the other. This doesn't mean, "You don't love me after all!" Or, "You don't satisfy me." More likely it means that expectations, tiredness, hormonal differences, fears, or past encounters have *temporarily* gotten in the way. These factors can be a source of conversation or a cause for prayer. But with God's help, you'll find a sexual balance.

Are you surprised that God is interested in your sex life? He created it, remember? And He can give you the words you need to tell your partner what you like—before you mention anything displeasing. Even if you feel embarrassed, you can say, "I like it when you _______." But don't stop there. Ask your mate what pleases him or her too. That's also your body now. You both have a right to find the appropriate time and way for your exclusive rights to lovemaking.

Prayer: Dear God, help us to get this right. We now have exclusive privileges to each other's bodies, right? Help us not to take advantage of or to forget Your rights in Jesus' name.

Journey with God: Give each other an exclusive interview about your sexual preferences. Ask God about the rights He's given you for the pleasure of each other's company.

Ah, you are beautiful, my love;
ah, you are beautiful;
your eyes are doves.
(Song of Solomon 1:15, NRSV)

Your exclusive rights as marriage partners allow you the privilege of saying things to one another that no one else can say without being out of line. In these first days of marriage, such "sweet talk" comes easily for most people. If that's not true for you, pray about it. The same God who inspired the sensuous Song of Solomon can give you the words your spouse most wants to hear.

Listen carefully, though, to the thoughts He brings to your mind because they might not be what you'd expected. For example, your mate has probably received compliments on some remarkable quality, but God may bring to your mind a trait, feature, or characteristic that's less noticeable. Suddenly, it may come to you to say, "I love the way your face lights when you smile." Or, "I could listen to your voice forever." Or, "Without perfume, you smell delicious."

If you're given to poetry—and even if you're not—you might find yourself creating fresh metaphor or simile. "Your skin is as _________ as __________. Your eyes are like a __________." Such poetic statements won't compare your spouse to another person but to something that describes him or her more fully.

You might prefer to speak figuratively or literally, but speak! Say what God brings to your mind. Also, listen to clues from your spouse about those areas where acceptance and love would be especially appreciated. Notice. Observe.

Although sexual awareness plays a big part in your first days of marriage, your honeymoon offers much more. This is a time for keen senses as you hear, smell, taste, touch, or feel what no one else will know about the person you married. Look. Listen. See through the soft, loving eyes of a dove.

Prayer: Dear Holy Father, thank You for Your Holy Spirit, Who descends like a dove on those who follow You. Help us to hear Your word of love as we speak to each other in Christ's name.

Journey with God: What beauty do you see in your mate's face, mannerisms, personality, or character? Write down what God helps you to notice, exclusively.

Day 11

My beloved speaks and says to me:
"Arise, my love, my fair one,
and come away."
(Song of Solomon 2:10, NRSV)

"Oh, I wish we could be alone together always!"

If you've had the good fortune to take a trip on your honeymoon, you've found time for each other exclusively. New or romantic surroundings helped you to shut out the rest of the world, so you could easily give one another continuous, complete attention.

Once you're back to work or school, you might find it's harder to "arise and come away" from everyday distractions and routines, but that doesn't mean the honeymoon is over! As you continue to have exclusive time together, you'll find it's just begun.

In this honeymoon period, you're getting to know each other with greater intimacy than you've ever had. You're learning about private matters in lovemaking, of course, but you're also becoming intimately acquainted with each other's hopes, goals, interests, and ways of doing or seeing things. This, too, is a discovery of your individual passions.

"I didn't know you felt that strongly about _________." Or, "You never told me this before."

Sometimes you might find yourselves staying up long hours, telling each other your secrets, memories, ambitions, or how something made you feel. With each telling moment, you discover more about this unique person you married! You give and receive a little more love, respect, empathy, and insight into what makes you the individuals you've become. In these times alone, you come away together—loved and BE-loved—into the marriage union and communion of passionately good friends.

Prayer: Oh, Lord, I don't want our honeymoon to end! Help us to keep our passion for one another and for life always in Christ's name.

Journey with God: What hopes, dreams, goals, or beliefs do you arduously embrace? Talk with God and your mate about the passionate interests you have.

On the third day a wedding took place at Cana in Galilee. Jesus' mother was there, and Jesus and his disciples had also been invited to the wedding.
(John 2:1–2, NIV)

As newlyweds, don't you just love hearing how Jesus' first recorded miracle occurred at a wedding? In case you haven't heard, that's where He turned water into wine—not just any wine, but wine better than the very best label!

If you're familiar with Bible stories, you'll recall how God's promises often began with a husband and wife, such as Adam and Eve, Abraham and Sarah, Elizabeth and Zechariah, Mary and Joseph. So it's not surprising that Jesus came into a love setting from the start. It's also not surprising that He attended the wedding in the close company of His mother and friends. But what's astonishing is this: Jesus was invited!

In these first days of marriage, you and your spouse have been inviting each other into your secrets, dreams, and goals. As you talk and listen, you begin to see what's really important to one another. Some hopes or preferences will be the same for both of you. Some will be so different, the other person hasn't even thought about them before! But when something really matters to one of you, it suddenly becomes important to both of you.

Is it really, really important to you to invite Christ into your marriage? If so, praise God! Then look for His leading to a church that provides you with the close company you're both to keep. Consider, where can you best witness the ongoing miracle and transforming power of Christ's Holy Spirit? Pray, where will you receive the wine?

Prayer: Heavenly Father, we invite You to come into our marriage and turn it into the very best one possible in Jesus' name.

Journey with God: To taste Christ's wine, start with water. If you haven't already done so, talk with God about baptism. Search His word to see what the Bible has to say. Discuss your church preferences with each other.

Come with me from Lebanon, my spouse, with me from Lebanon: look from the top of Amana, from the top of Shenir and Hermon, from the lions' dens, from the mountains of the leopards.
(Song of Solomon 4:8, KJV)

Being in love brings euphoria. Being in wedded love brings the setting for an ongoing honeymoon!

As you confide your hopes, beliefs, and desires in each other, you'll discover that your experiences don't always overlap. You won't have a perfect match of backgrounds or viewpoints. But as you listen to one another, you'll both have a bigger honeymoon with life!

Say, for instance, your spouse has a constricted view of Christianity. He or she may not be able to see how a person's confession, baptism, and communion fit in until you lovingly tell how you see it. Or say an unfortunate incident made your mate hesitant about churchgoing. If so, you can acknowledge that, then show the view you found.

As you look through each other's experiences, you'll be able to perceive what you hadn't yet noticed or understood. You might see how churches consist of imperfect but *forgiven* people, perfected by Jesus Christ. (That's Good News —and an outlook worth sharing!) Or you might see how customs color each denomination's beliefs without blocking the overall view of worshiping God and proclaiming Christ as Savior.

Because you're still individuals, you'll each have your preferences. You'll each present what's comfortable to you as you seek a church home. So, don't be afraid to go up on a mountain to see each other's denominational terrain. The climb may be hard at first, but when you reach the summit you'll be blessed to have your spouse with you as you both enjoy the holy, breath-giving view!

Prayer: Dear Father, please help us to have the strength and courage to climb out of our own familiar views and into Your vision of the Church in Jesus' name.

Journey with God: Talk with God about the rough terrain or past falls either of you has experienced on the religious scene. Pray for His panoramic view to expand before you.

Day 14

I delight greatly in the Lord;
my soul rejoices in my God.
For he has clothed me with garments
of salvation and arrayed me in
a robe of righteousness,
as a bridegroom adorns his head
like a priest, and as a bride
adorns herself with her jewels.
(Isaiah 61:10, NIV)

Have the pictures of your wedding come back yet? Did you wear a beautifully flowing, white gown or a dashing tuxedo? If so, you probably spent weeks finding just what you wanted. Then you made the arrangements and spent more time going to fittings until your attire fit perfectly. Or maybe you just had a fit, trying to decide what to wear!

Elaborately or modestly, formally or informally, you dressed up in some way for your wedding. Your special attire added to the special occasion and, hopefully, made it picture perfect. Regardless, you won't like every photograph you see. Some will seem terrific, others terrible. But, hey! That's how people really are.

That's how you are too. Some days you're at your best in looks, energy, wits, and mood. Some days your hair, feet, or thoughts straggle, or you slam a door to accentuate your frame of mind. Neither of you consistently looks like the flawless bride or groom atop a wedding cake. If you did, you'd be made out of plastic.

Into that realistic, everyday picture Christ comes. Invited, He saves the occasion, rescues the mood, restores the energy, reproves the thought, and recounts the number and placement of every hair on your head! He knows you. He takes you out of the darkroom to restore and complete you. Given opportunities throughout the process, He fully develops you into a wondrous picture of Himself.

Prayer: Dear Heavenly Father, sometimes I don't like seeing closeups of me. Thanks for bringing Jesus into the picture!

Journey with God: Were you hoping your wedding photos would make you seem flawless? You are! As you confess an imperfect word, thought, or deed and seek forgiveness, you wear Christ's righteousness. So see what needs confessing and forgiving.

Catch us the foxes, the little foxes, that ruin the vineyards—for our vineyards are in blossom.
(Song of Solomon 2:15, NRSV)

The more picturesque your wedding, the more rushing around you probably did beforehand. Maybe you had a lengthy honeymoon to recuperate, but quite possibly the activities made you more tired. Much too soon, you both had to resume your everyday routines, and that automatically put additional strain on your private time together.

Into a blossoming honeymoon, little foxes like to creep. Sometimes you see them coming. Sometimes not, but they're there. They're not a big crisis or an obvious concern. No, they're the small, pesky things that divert your attention from one another or nibble at your romance.

Look around and you might see a little fox while it's still a cub. Has a minor worry been capturing your thoughts? Has a problem at work or school kept you from being around your spouse, even when you seem to be there in person? Has a bad attitude or tiny dissatisfaction taken teeny bites from the fruits of love, joy, and peace? Has something snatched any blossoms of romance from your marriage?

When you see a little fox coming toward you or your spouse, don't club it to death. But, in Jesus' name, quickly shoo it away. Protect precious intervals together by handling small concerns promptly so they won't devour time, energy, or thought. Don't let pesky matters ruin your ongoing honeymoon.

Prayer: Heavenly Father, we need Your discernment before we can even know what's nibbling away at us in body, mind, or spirit. Help us to stay lovingly aware of each other and be on guard against anything that threatens our inner peace or time together. Please nurture us and help our marriage to flourish with the fruit of Your spirit in Jesus' name.

Journey with God: List any worrisome or annoying areas that have been sneaking in to steal love, joy, and peace from you or your spouse. Discuss these together—with God.

Day 16

He brought me to the banqueting house, and his banner over me was love.
(Song of Solomon 2:4, KJV)

Heard any good in-law jokes lately? If so, they might not seem too funny. If you're having trouble adjusting to your mother or father-in-law (and vice versa), you might feel more like crying.

Here's how it is: Parents invest exorbitant amounts of time, energy, attention, training, hope, and love into their children, not to mention money. They put in countless hours of thankless, exhausting, and sometimes mindless tasks—feeding, tending, clothing, housing, leading, and following their child around. Then, suddenly, it stops.

That's where you came in. Just when mom or dad wondered what to do with themselves, you showed up and took on many of their prior concerns. Some days they want to thank you for caring so much about their child. Other days, they just wish they could have their baby back again!

If you're the same sex as an in-law who causes you the most grief, don't be surprised by what's happening. Although it's a first for you, it isn't new. In many families, little jealousies creep in, so just expect that and consider how you would feel in your in-law's displaced place. Make a point of showing love and respect. And keep in-laws in prayer!

If you're the person who's married to the person who has a personal problem with the person who raised you, you can do even more, personally, to help! When you're in the company of folks you grew up with, you can show clear evidence of affection and loyalty toward your spouse. You can raise a banner of love around your husband or wife so everyone can easily see it.

Prayer: Dear Lord, please help us to demonstrate Your love for each other in the law and love of Jesus' name.

Journey with God: A banner shows what team you're on. Have you shown your husband, wife, parents, siblings, employer, close friends, and in-laws that your first commitment is to God and then your spouse? Talk with God and your mate about appropriate ways you can make this lovingly apparent.

Set me as a seal upon thine heart,
as a seal upon thine arm:
for love is strong as death;
jealousy is cruel as the grave;
the coals thereof are coals of fire,
which hath a most vehement flame.
(Song of Solomon 8:6, KJV*)*

Who would have thought it? The Bible advocates wearing your heart on your sleeve! Often, the world makes fun of true affection. A parent, brother, sister, employer, church member, or childhood friend might tease or, playfully, give you a hard time. Maybe they'll even break into a chorus of "True Love" or ask why you forgot to wear your nose ring.

Because you're still newlyweds, you can expect people to tease you as they ease through their own awkwardness. It's not that they're sitting around thinking about how you're having sex. (Okay, maybe they are.) They're trying to find a way to acknowledge a change of status and also make some adjustments in their relationship with you.

People you've probably known longer than your spouse have been displaced somewhat. With your marriage partner to consider, you're not always free to get together with someone else. So the closer you were to this other person, the more threatened he or she might feel.

Meanwhile, your husband or wife has similar feelings—especially if you don't have a lengthy history together. As long as you're alone, your spouse probably feels confident in your love. But what happens when you're around other people? Do you show your spouse supportive love that everyone can see?

Romantic love belongs in private, of course, but in public you can be consistent about giving your spouse appropriate attention. This keeps jealousy from arising and also helps to strengthen your marriage pact. So seal that pact with love! Keep your regard for one another evident and, when needed, wear your heart on your sleeve.

Prayer: Heavenly Father, in public or in private, help us to be supportive of each other in Jesus' name.

Journey with God: Ask God to help you show loyalty to each other at all times. Take note of what you hear.

Let us rejoice and be glad and give him glory! For the wedding of the Lamb has come, and his bride has made herself ready.
(Revelation 19:7, NIV)

Did you get married without telling anyone? If so, tell them now! Send wedding announcements to everyone you know who would be interested in hearing your good news. The list might include favorite childhood friends or neighbors, out-of-town friends and relatives, or anyone who's prayed for you to find just the right spouse.

Place a wedding announcement and photograph in your hometown newspapers and local paper too. If the church you grew up in has a monthly newsletter or weekly bulletin, phone the church office. Call anyone who will be happy for you.

If, however, you planned your wedding months in advance, the people closest to you probably know you're married, but don't assume they do. Let them know! Let them rejoice with you. Otherwise, you'll feel bad when you don't hear from someone you had hoped would acknowledge your marriage. People do have a tendency to forget. Besides, if the actual service has been a long time in coming, everyone might think you're oldyweds by now.

People seem to think that about Christ and His Bride. Instead of getting ready for the Lord with eager, loving anticipation, they have a tendency to forget that He's coming again. They act as though religion fits them like an old hat instead of a wedding veil.

Because your own wedding is so recent, you're thinking about announcing your news to everyone who will rejoice with you. But even if the ceremony seems like a long time in coming, don't forget to announce, rejoice in, and make yourself ready for the Church's marriage to Jesus Christ.

Prayer: Dear Heavenly Father, thank You for giving us people who rejoice in the announcement of our marriage. Thank You for wedding us in Jesus' holy name.

Journey with God: Without meaning to, have you kept your marriage a secret? Make a list of those you want to know about your good news. Ask God who to tell about the Good News of your marriage to Him.

The voice of joy and the voice of gladness, the voice of the bridegroom and the voice of the bride, the voice of those who sing as they bring sacrifices of thanksgiving into the house of the Lord. Give praise and thanks to the Lord of hosts for the Lord is good.
(Jeremiah 33:11a, AMP)

Aren't you glad to have so many friends and relatives to give you wedding gifts! These presents *present* you with basic items and pretty things for starting your new household. Now you won't have to run buy a crockpot—especially if you've already gotten three!

Although you'll usually be glad when you first receive an item, you might not be as thankful the second or third time around. You might not appreciate the ugly vase or weird-looking lamp someone sent. And you'll probably wish those new towels and linens didn't clash with your color scheme.

Sometimes you won't be too glad about what you're given—whether a gift from other people, one another, or from God. Sometimes you'll feel offended, upset, or just plain annoyed. But even in those situations you'll be glad to know you can purposely offer a "sacrifice of praise."

When you don't like the gifts you've received, you can still be thankful that friends or relatives thought of you and spent time or money selecting something they hoped you would enjoy. You can still write thank-you notes, acknowledging each present and the generosity of its giver. You can still be glad people care about you, and be quick to let them know.

Your Heavenly Father cares about you always. So if a circumstance, situation, or gift doesn't please you, you can still be prompt about offering praise. Give thanks to God—even if it seems like a really big sacrifice at the time.

Prayer: Dear Father, forgive us for complaining or making fun of good gifts from friends and relatives or from You. Help us to accept the love and caring we're shown and offer You our ongoing thanks in Jesus' name.

Journey with God: Ask God what word of thanksgiving He'd like you to write in each thank-you note. Include praise of Him!

However, each one of you also must love his wife as he loves himself, and the wife must respect her husband.
(Ephesians 5:33, NIV)

Having a loving husband and a respectable, respectful wife certainly gives you both cause for thanksgiving. But in your first weeks as newlyweds you might not be terribly thankful about some of the unpleasantries marriage brings! As you notice traits and habits about each other that you don't particularly like, reality sets in.

One of you takes all the covers, leaves the milk setting out, scatters dirty clothes on the floor, clutters the living room, or leaves the toilet lid up in the middle of the night. Quite possibly one of you snores!

Sometimes snoring can be lessened by finding a pillow that won't let the chin drop or by avoiding allergens that create sinus congestion. Other times, there's nothing you can do. Usually, though, you and your spouse can *choose* to discard old habits. Then you're free to establish new ones together.

To marriage you both bring your upbringing! But because you love your wife and respect your husband, you won't be hindered by how you used to do something. You haven't yet had time to say, "That's how we do it in our family." You're a new family now. You're just beginning to create new patterns as a new gift for each other.

As you develop new habits, consider what can be improved or changed and discuss possible solutions. Adjust yourselves to differences in your background. Show love and respect by your willingness to exchange any unpleasant habits for the new ones really needed for married life.

Prayer: Heavenly Father, we confess to having habits that get on each other's nerves. Help us to find reasonable, workable solutions in Jesus' name.

Journey with God: Has your spouse asked you to do—or *not* to do—something that you *can* correct? List poor habits, but make a daily habit of talking with God.

Pray at all times (on every occasion, in every season) in the Spirit, with all [manner of] prayer and entreaty. To that end keep alert and watch with strong purpose and perseverance, interceding in behalf of all the saints (God's consecrated people).

(Ephesians 6:18, AMP*)*

"Have you seen my keys?"

"I thought you found them under the sofa cushion."

"Uh-uh, that was yesterday."

Determination doesn't make every bad habit disappear. You or your spouse might still have trouble finding keys, time, money, or something else you meant to hang onto. Maybe you think you're doing the best you can and simply cannot do any better. But with God's help, nothing is impossible.

The first step toward a change of habit, trait, attitude, or almost anything comes when you recognize that a problem or a need exists. Once you've specifically identified a concern, you can focus on it, not to fuss at yourself or your spouse, but to consider alternatives, prayerfully.

As you bring a concern to God, ask Him to block every thought from your mind but His. Then listen to what He has to say. Most likely you won't hear an audible voice, but you might have a new thought, fresh insight, or relevant Bible verse come to mind. Perhaps you'll suddenly have a clear impression of a course of action you're to take.

As you hear from God in each situation, ask Him to give you His prayers to pray. Then offer those to Him with your thanksgiving, petition, and praise. He's right there with you. So draw mightily from the Almighty! And don't hesitate to ask, "Lord, where did I put those keys?"

Prayer: Dear Heavenly Father, help us to know what needs correcting in our lives. Help us to see Your key for change in Jesus' name.

Journey with God: Are you praying on every occasion about all manner of things? Are you praying daily for each other? Talk about immediate concerns, and let God guide each request.

When angry, do not sin; do not ever let your wrath (your exasperation, your fury or indignation) last until the sun goes down. Leave no [such] room or foothold for the devil [give no opportunity to him].
(Ephesians 4:26, AMP)

When something goes badly or old habits get in the way, you might not even think to pray. Depending on your personality, the first thing that comes to your mind will be thoughts of what happened and how you feel—hurt or angry. But, surely, sometime before the sun goes down, you will remember, "Oh, I didn't pray about this!"

As soon as that thought occurs to you, do it! Having a word with God immediately squeezes out unproductive thoughts or attitudes. With your mind on prayer, there's no room for you to dwell in hurt nor space for adding to your anger by mentally replaying the episode again and again.

Instead of building hurt or anger against yourself or your spouse, prayer gives you opportunity to tell God how you feel. Once you've done this, respectfully, He enables you to hear His thoughts, view, or counsel. You'll feel calmer, and, in this listening side of prayer, you'll remember to forgive.

Over time, prayer also loosens the hold of those habits that lead you into upsets. As you ask God to help you with a harmful pattern, you let go of whatever you're holding onto—whether it's a grudge, grief, wound, or indignation.

God then brings His power into the situation. Tempers quieten. Pains soften. Faith builds. And you feel better, too!

As you ask God's help for your spouse, you also discover His insight to guide your prayers. Maybe you'll see that a habit doesn't matter after all. But if something does need to change, praying helps you to demonstrate love and respect for your spouse. You show, "I'm in this with you," as you become evenly tempered, together, in the Lord.

Prayer: Dear God, please help us to let go of hurt or anger so we can better accept each other and You in Jesus' name.

Journey with God: Do you suspect you're too easily riled or wounded? Do you often let go of tears or temper? Let God temper both of you as you seek Him in prayer together.

Day 23

Let there be no filthiness (obscenity, indecency) nor foolish and sinful (silly and corrupt) talk, nor coarse jesting, which are not fitting or becoming; but instead voice your thankfulness [to God].

(Ephesians 5:4, AMP)

"Oops! Did I say that?"

Have you noticed how contagious foul language is? Once started, foulish talk spreads like chicken pox! If you or your spouse catch it, apply prayer liberally. Also consider: It just might be called "foul" language because people use it when they're too chicken to say what they really mean!

As you prayerfully freshen the language in your house, let each other know what you find especially offensive. If a certain tone, gesture, phrase, remark, or attitude bothers you, say so. No explanations are needed. Let it be enough to say, "I don't like to hear that," or, "To me that's obscene."

Usually, foul language includes "barnyard words," "swear words," or cursing. However, the worse talk may, on the surface, seem fine. Like an infestation of unseen and deadly germs, foolish, sinful talk puts a spouse down.

Speaking ill—even in jest—of your life's partner is obscene, coarse, indecent, unfitting, and unbecoming to you both. Conversely, conversation that's appropriate boosts your spouse's mood, hopes, humor, self-confidence, and spirits. So, either way, the words you say will help or hinder, heal or hurt both of you. They can lighten or darken a mood. They can uplift or bring down a spirit.

Don't, however, be afraid to say anything. Your spouse can't know what you really think unless you speak. So if you see a helpful need for change, say so. If you have uplifting thoughts, speak up. Give voice to your love and respect for each other by using relevant, timely, and precisely fitting words of thanksgiving, praise, and prayer.

Prayer: Heavenly Father, sometimes we're quick to say what we don't like but slow about saying what we appreciate or enjoy about each other and You. Forgive us, Lord. Help us to praise You and upbuild one another in Jesus' name.

Journey with God: With God's help, talk about how you talk.

Day 24

Therefore do not be vague and thoughtless and foolish, but understanding and firmly grasping what the will of the Lord is.
(Ephesians 5:17, AMP)

In this busy society, couples often misunderstand one another because they don't take time to talk things through. That doesn't mean you have to work things out by staying up all night! But it does mean being more specific as you communicate what you think or feel.

Families often talk in code. People use gestures or pet phrases. They make vague statements or broad assumptions and give vent to emotions that cloud, rather than clarify, the issue. Sometimes this happens accidentally. Sometimes it's a way to avoid taking responsibility for what the person really means.

If verbal haze hangs over your home like environmental waste, ask God to clear the air. Set your minds and hearts to work on cleaning up the situation with clear communication that filters the debris. To do that, first think. Find out exactly what's bothering you. Then state the facts as you see them, being precise, concise, specific, and fair.

In an unexpected or highly emotional situation, however, neither of you will know what you think at first. So give each other time. To hear yourself and God better, take a walk by yourself or a long soak in the tub. Pray about whatever is troubling you and listen to the clear thoughts God brings to your mind.

As you begin to see what you really think, you and your spouse might disagree. Whether your thoughts coincide or not, however, you can agree to find out what God thinks. He'll give you an inner word or assurance as needed. But He's already spoken His will and collected His thoughts in His word.

Prayer: Dear God, thank You for speaking to us clearly in Your word. Help us to grasp what You say in Jesus' name.

Journey with God: Do you feel confused about what you're even supposed to think? Learn what God thinks. Reading the Bible, cover to cover, takes no more time than it does to read any book of that length. Discuss a daily schedule for reading the Bible. Make plans to discover God's thoughts together.

But now in Christ Jesus,
you who once were [so] far away,
through (by, in) the blood of
Christ have been brought near.
For He is [Himself] our peace
(our bond of unity and harmony).
(Ephesians 2:13–14a, AMP)

As you get to know God and His word better, you may be in for a shock! You might discover that some of the sayings you've heard all of your life and even tried to copy didn't come from the Bible at all. They might have come from the classics, a movie, or an example set by someone you admired. They sounded good, but now you find they're the exact opposite of what the Bible says.

As you get to know yourselves better, you might also be surprised to see that some very good things about you differ too. Maybe you don't share the same view on politics, health, education, art, music, or moral issues. Or maybe it's more personal. Maybe a standard that's quite obvious to you or a goal that's important makes no sense at all to your spouse.

To this confusion, add two separate upbringings, two different perspectives, two sets of character traits, and two members of the opposite sex. Since opposites frequently do attract, you might wonder how you'll ever get along!

If you didn't love and respect each other, you wouldn't! However, with the motion and commotion in today's world, loving and respecting each other isn't always enough. You want more. You need more. You need God. You need prayer. You need Jesus Christ to bring you together, harmoniously, into His view.

Throughout married life you'll experience times when your differences make you distant. But even when you seem hopelessly far away, in spirit or in truth, you can look to God to bring you back together. You then find the opposite of distance. You find the greatest intimacy possible in any relationship as you *pray* together in Christ's name.

Prayer: Forgive us for saying so, Lord, but we're embarrassed to pray aloud together. Help us to cross beyond our feelings and differences so we can be wholly united in Jesus' name.

Journey with God: In what ways do you need Christ's peace? As God brings troubled areas to mind, pray about them together.

Rather, let our lives lovingly express truth [in all things speaking truly, dealing truly, living truly]. Enfolded in love, let us grow up in every way and in all things into Him Who is the Head, [even] Christ (the Messiah, the Anointed One).

(Ephesians 4:15, AMP)

Will power! Because you love each other, you have lots of will power—the willingness needed to power a change of habits, preferences, or routines.

For instance, if one of you loves broccoli, the other might be willing to try. If one of you likes to play tennis, the other will give it all the power he or she can put into a game. If one of you wants to get involved in a couples Bible study, the other will cooperate willingly. If both of you favor sleeping on the right side of the bed, one of you will take what's left!

Your affection encourages you to cooperate. This means you will adapt your schedules, habits, and any other area you can readily adjust or change. However, true love respectfully requires you to accept yourselves as you are, not necessarily as your partner wants you to be.

If one of you has ever asked your spouse, "Tell me what you want me to be," you've asked the wrong person! Don't ask your husband or wife. Ask God. He made you the individual you are. He created your looks, brains, talents, abilities, and personality. He doesn't want anyone to hinder what He's begun, so don't change His creation for your spouse.

God wants you to grow up, but not into someone who isn't you. He wants you to mature into the person you truly are—full grown in His will. He wants you to know what He would have you be—fully enfolded in His love.

Prayer: Dear Heavenly Father, forgive us for the times we've been dissatisfied with ourselves or each other as the persons you created. Help us to grow up in You in Jesus' name.

Journey with God: Are you looking to your spouse or other people to tell you who you are? Look to God. Listen and take note of His truths for you.

Day 27

And be constantly renewed in the spirit of your mind [having a fresh mental and spiritual attitude].
(Ephesians 4:23, AMP)

Most couples come to marriage with expectations of what a husband or wife should be. Sometimes a hope, a fantasy, a dream, or even a misconception turns into a desire you think marriage will fulfill. However, people often expect a spouse to be just like mom or dad!

If, for instance, your father used to say each night, "That was a good dinner," you'll expect your spouse to do the same when you cook a meal. If that doesn't happen, you'll be disappointed. Or, if your mother believed that "Good books make good friends," you'll expect your spouse to value bookshelves and library cards. If he or she couldn't care less, you might wonder what's wrong with that person. But what's really wrong is placing those expectations on anyone in the first place.

Already you've begun to discover your differences. Now you'll see you're quite different from each other's parents too. What worked for them as individuals or as a married couple might not even be realistic for either or both of you.

When you first see a difference between your hopes and reality, you might feel somewhat disappointed. But as you relinquish expectations, you're free to make new discoveries and surprises about each other. Oh, your spouse might forget to acknowledge a meal or read a book, but he or she has other surprisingly wonderful gifts you'd never thought to expect.

So as you become more intimately acquainted, be open to receive. Keep a fresh outlook—one that continuously renews your faith in your spouse, yourself, and God. Don't expect anything. But expectantly await every good thing God brings.

Prayer: Heavenly Father, thank You for renewing our minds and spirit in the power of Jesus' name.

Journey with God: Be honest. What did you really expect out of marriage? Talk with God about any areas of disappointment and release your expectations to Him.

For the husband is the head of the wife as Christ is the head of the church, his body, of which he is the Savior.
(Ephesians 5:23, NIV)

If you're used to being on your own, you've probably noticed that the first weeks of marriage include a power play. Before marriage, you had the enjoyment of making your own decisions and, within reason, doing what you liked. Maybe you expected that to continue, but don't count on it!

Each of you has your own personality, priorities, and preferences, so conflicts will occur. You want your way. Your spouse wants his or her way, and you both want the final say. Clearly, someone needs to be in charge, but who?

In these first weeks you both need to know that hubby gets the job. God's word establishes him as the head of the household, not because he's good, better, or best, but because he's immediately responsible for every choice within your family. He's the first one accountable to the Head Supervisor—the Husband and Head of the Church, Jesus Christ.

That's just how it is, biblically speaking. Yet, thanks be to God, this works in a practical sense too. At first that's hard to see—especially when your family includes only two people. It seems as though both of you should have an equal say or, perhaps, take turns making decisions. But because differences occur and each choice involves you both, one person needs to take the lead in your family to keep you from going in equal but separate directions.

To keep yourselves together, just remember: Jesus Christ is the One to whom you'll both hand in your accounts. He's the One God ultimately placed in charge. So give Him the power. Let Him have His way.

Prayer: Dear Lord, please take charge of our family. Thanks!

Journey with God: Both of you have the job of reporting daily to the Lord for instructions. Talk with your spouse about what you hear. Let Christ save you from going in opposite directions.

Now as the church submits to Christ, so also wives should submit to their husbands in everything.
(Ephesians 5:24, NIV)

If you've ever thought of submission as another word for doormat, think again! Anyone who knows Christ well knows He would never walk all over His bride, the Church. But He can be counted on, as the bridegroom, to *groom* His bride.

To groom means to dress up, make ready, comb out, and even adorn with jewels. But that won't happen unless the bride submits herself to the process of being gussied up. Then, wow! What a transformation! It's like Cinderella going from self-absorbent, ragged edges into the finery of love.

As a wife practices submission to her husband, strange things start to happen: She submits her thoughts to him, so he has the benefit of another point of view. She submits her feelings, giving him opportunity to sense emotions beyond his own experience. She submits her hopes and dreams, and he sees new possibilities. She submits her beliefs in the man she married, and he begins to believe in himself more.

In this give-and-take relationship, something rises from the cinders to take a wondrous shape. The woman becomes so well groomed in communicative love and submissive persuasion, she begins to behave like a church. And the man? He listens so well and takes such appropriate, responsive action to his helpmeet's prayerful requests, he begins to think, act, look, and love more and more like Jesus.

Prayer: Heavenly Father, we have a long way to go. We don't seem very Christlike or churchlike. Helps us to submit our thoughts, words, and actions to You in Jesus' name.

Journey with God: In this space, write down every word God brings to your minds about the persuasive influence and holy, powerful purpose of His Church. Then write what comes to you about the loving, protective, grooming power of Jesus Christ. When you've completed the list, talk about the fitting traits you already see in each other as the Lord prepares you both for Christlike, churchlike service in His name.

Let the wife see that she respects and reverences her husband [that she notices him, regards him, honors him, prefers him, venerates, and esteems him; and that she defers to him, praises him, and loves and admires him exceedingly].

(Ephesians 5:33b, AMP)

Have you found a church home you both like? As you think about the qualities you want to find in a church, each of you will have specific preferences.

For instance, one of you might like a place where people seem to enjoy fellowship with each other and where they also welcome you. Or perhaps you want a church that's involved in helping society through strong outreach programs or in aiding individuals through Christlike counseling. If you have the same denominational background, you might prefer a church that's familiar and aligns with your theology. Maybe you just want to hear great sermons from an excellent pastor.

Those are good reasons to enjoy a church, but not reason enough to join. The first priority needs to be a place where both of you can *worship* God. This means finding a church that helps you notice, regard, honor, prefer, venerate, esteem, defer to, praise, love, and exceedingly admire the Lord.

As a Christian wife, you have a similar priority. No, you won't worship the ground your husband walks on. But you will defer to him as the head of your family. You'll love and admire him, even if you don't always understand what he's doing. You'll consistently commend his talents and abilities to other people, speaking of him in a positive way and showing faith in him. You'll treat him with such notice, regard, honor, praise, preference, and esteem that, over the years, he just might begin to love you and your company even more than he does right now.

Prayer: Dear God, help us to upbuild and uphold one another, worshiping only You in Jesus' name.

Journey with God: As church representatives for your family, learn more about the Christian family you represent. Ask your husband what he likes you to notice and how he wants you to defer to him. Discuss these questions and answers with God.

Day 31

Husbands, love your wives [be affectionate and sympathetic with them] and do not be harsh or bitter or resentful toward them.
(Colossians 3:19, AMP)

So have you had your first argument? Who won? Unless you kissed and made up, no one did. But there's more than that to a fair fight.

When you disagree, several things happen: Each of you brings your upbringing, beliefs, opinions, viewpoint, and the facts as you see them. If a sharp difference occurs, you each bring your emotions too.

"Why on earth would you want to do that?"

"That's what I'm trying to tell you!"

The more solid a stance either of you takes, the more unlikely the other person will be to win you over to his or her side. So where does that leave you? Beside yourself, or somewhere outside the relationship, waiting! At least one of you (perhaps both) will also be somewhere outside God's will for your family.

Did either of you forget? You *are* a family. You're one. In that God-inspired, God-ordained marriage setting, both of you remain individually accountable. However, as a couple, both of you still count. Both of you have thoughts, feelings, and legitimate points of view. Both of you have hopes, plans, goals, and beliefs that will certainly affect the other in some way. Both of you also have an ongoing responsibility to listen and to respond to one another with respect and love.

Maybe you'll agree. Maybe you won't. But look for a solution that won't leave a bitter residue on the tip of your tongue just waiting to spew acidic remarks. Kiss and make up. Beyond the sympathetic hug and affectionate kiss, forgiveness comes for you to savor. A flavor of understanding may follow love's sweet taste.

Prayer: Dear God, please bring us together in Christ's name.

Journey with God: Does arguing your viewpoint make you withhold your affection and any sympathy toward your spouse's view? Ask God how to show love and respect during a debate!

Be subject to one another out of reverence for Christ.
(Ephesians 5:21, NRSV)

Can you see a Christlike pattern for your marriage? Have you noticed that it continuously involves submitting your love and respect to one another? Well, sometimes the need for submission isn't quite what it seems!

Say, for instance, a couple has a difference of opinion. Certain that he's right, the husband submits his logical view for consideration. The wife, knowing that she's to defer to him, accepts what's said without submitting her concerns about the matter, or without saying what she wants and how this makes her feel. Ironically, in her quickness to defer to her husband's opinion, she doesn't *submit* anything.

Or say the wife does offer her thoughts, reservations, or insights about a decision that will affect them both. She states how she feels but shows her husband respect by letting him choose. If he does so without showing any acknowledgment or regard for what she's said, he's submitted his opinion or decision but not much evidence of his love.

So what's your verdict? Can you see that how you feel about something won't make much difference unless you submit that information to your spouse? It's like withholding all evidence of your thoughts, perceptions, or beliefs. You must first hand them over. You must offer, give up, and let go of what you submit. Otherwise you withhold your true self and genuine thoughts or feelings from the very person you love.

Being subject to each other makes you both open—and vulnerable. But in reverence to Christ, you can trust your spouse enough to submit evidence of caring. Lovingly and respectfully, you can get your heads and hearts together to discover the whole truth in Christ—the Head and Heart of every matter in your home.

Prayer: Dear God, please help us to submit ourselves, wholly, to one another in Jesus' name.

Journey with God: Have you submitted half-truths, innuendoes, or barbed retorts to your spouse? Ask God to help you testify in love and truth on behalf of yourself, your spouse, and Him.

Now there are diversities of gifts,
but the same Spirit.
(1 Corinthians 12:4, KJV)

"Look at the new painting I just bought. Won't it look great over the sofa?"

"It'd look better over the garbage disposal."

Being subject to one another makes your tastes subject to your spouse's approval—or disapproval. Therefore, you'll have less conflicts over decor if you agree on a purchase before it's made.

As you discuss what you want in your home, consider your individual tastes. For example, if one of you likes yellow and the other blue, you might find fabrics that bring shades of those two colors together. If your tastes clash violently, just select a neutral beige or gray to use throughout your home. Then confine the conflicting colors to accents, such as pillows or paintings, that you'll place in separate rooms.

Besides taste in colors, discuss samples of the lifestyle you prefer. For example, if you like to sprawl in front of a television, that's probably not the room for a Victorian love seat. If you have a career or other involvement that often requires you to entertain, it won't work too well to have a roomful of recliners. (An empty room with folding chairs, maybe . . .)

This is your home! Whether you rent or buy, it belongs to both of you, so let the place reflect the mood or personal environment you want to create for yourselves. If your tastes don't blend at all, mix them for an eclectic look.

God knows all about variety. A glimpse at nature shows diversity in His creation—including you. That's exciting, sometimes challenging, but seldom boring. So discover the varied gifts, tastes, and talents God has given both of you. Enjoy them. Value them. Welcome them. Make room for them—and each other—in the Lord.

Prayer: Dear Heavenly Father, thank You for the wonderful variety You bring to us. Help us to appreciate every gift of Your spirit that we've received in Jesus' name.

Journey with God: List what you'd like in your home. Ask God to combine your personalities and tastes in His spirit.

Day 34

But lay up for yourselves treasures in heaven, where neither moth nor rust doth corrupt, and where thieves do not break through nor steal: For where your treasure is, there will your heart be also.
(Matthew 6:20–21, KJV)

How well do your spending tastes match? If you think just alike on money matters, you probably won't argue about the subject, but you could be in a bind. If both of you save every penny, neither might point out, "But we *have* to buy this!" Or, if you both share a motto, "Spend! Spend!" the one who says, "Whoa! Stop!" may be the company who issued your credit cards!

Whether you have one source of income or a dozen, pray about your tastes in spending. Consider your long-range goals and what you hope to accomplish financially. For instance, if one of you needs something crucial, such as job training or medical attention, take that expense into account before you purchase costly items like a new carpet or car.

How you spend your money shows what's important to you. At first, material things may seem to have more value than you'd like, especially if you need to buy furniture or major appliances. Even then, just look for quality second-hand items at a good price. Or wait for sales. If you're not sure how long a wait that will be, ask a store clerk when their best annual sales occur—probably when new models come out.

As you consider making purchases for your home or taking care of special needs, let each other know what you cherish. For instance, you might want to travel or have a garden or play uplifting music—all of which cost money but provide memorable times nothing can steal. If you see the value of Bible reading, don't get rusty in your knowledge of its contents. Buy your favorite version in a leather-bound copy that can endure daily use throughout the years. With that treasure, surely your heart will follow along as you read.

Prayer: Dear Lord, please help us to value what's pleasing to You as expressed in Your word in Jesus' name.

Journey with God: What treasures cost money but offer much more than money can buy? Make a list of what's important to you, and discuss those preferences with each other and God.

For the love of money is a root of all kinds of evils; it is through this craving that some have been led astray and have wandered from the faith and pierced themselves through with many acute [mental] pains.

(2 Timothy 6:10, AMP)

Don't you just love having lots of money to spend? Most people do, but you'll be happy to know that's not the same as loving the stuff of which a purchase is made.

For some, money becomes their goal. They seek people, contacts, places, or careers they don't like, just to build their financial worth. They go where the money is, even if they hate living or working in that location. They agree to duties they despise or tasks they know are wrong. They sell what they are and what they believe in simply because that's how much their treasure costs.

The first time your mailbox fills with monthly bills, you might be tempted to sell out too. You might feel swayed toward treasuring money more than you'd intended. You might find yourselves thinking about options you wouldn't otherwise consider. And if there's a big discrepancy between what you owe and what you have, you might feel some acute mental pain.

You'll really feel anguished if you forget to balance your checkbook and discover you're overdrawn. If so, it won't help to lead your spouse astray by letting him or her think everything is fine. An apology to your husband or wife and arrangements with your creditors will keep you from wandering into debt and getting rooted there. So be honest with your spouse, your creditors, and yourself. Face the truth about money with God, the One who truly provides for your family.

Prayer: Heavenly Father, somehow we added earnings together but forgot to subtract anything. Please forgive our poor choices in spending. Help us to balance each other and our resources well in Jesus' name.

Journey with God: Do you have a realistic monthly budget? Ask God to help you establish one together as you list your immediate needs and ongoing expenses in this space.

Day 36

No one can serve two masters.
Either he will hate the one and
love the other, or he will be devoted
to the one and despise the other.
You cannot serve both
God and Money.
(Matthew 6:24, NIV*)*

Did your monthly budget refuse to budge? Did you have to adapt your spending tastes to a medicinal dose of reality? Do you feel confused about money matters? Have you prayed about these concerns together?

Before you try to balance your budget, pray together first. Start by seeking God's presence. Ask Him (1) to guide your conversation, (2) help you to see each other's view or needs, and (3) remind you both to take into account your long and short-term goals. If, however, you decide not to invite God into your discussion about finances, don't be surprised if He skips the meeting.

No one can serve two masters. If bad spending habits, money worries, debts, or plain old greed start to master you, God will get out of the way and let you serve yourself. Of course, you wouldn't be reading this if you wanted Him to bow out completely. Yet, without realizing it, you could be expecting God to bow or yield to your monetary desires.

Aren't you glad He won't? It's not that He doesn't care about you or that He can't afford your expensive tastes. He's God. He owns the whole universe and all its resources. So trust Him, listen to Him, and obey the instructions He puts on your heart and mind. Then count on Him to give you what's needed.

When you choose God as your Master, you allow Him to manage your finances according to His priorities. He won't write your checks or pay your phone bill. But He will reveal the ways your money can better serve you and Him.

Prayer: Dear God, we praise Your wealth of knowledge, wisdom, and material goods too. Thank You for showing us how to serve You and keep money subservient. Thank You that we can always count on You in Jesus' name.

Journey with God: Have you depended on God or money to help you, financially? Instead of relying on cash or credit, write your personal IOU for serving God.

Day 37

Many waters cannot quench love,
neither can floods drown it.
If one offered for love all
the wealth of his house,
it would be utterly scorned.
(Song of Solomon 8:7, NRSV)

Love or money? When you decide to put God first, love stays on your side. After all, it's on His. God is love. So adoration, affection, attachment, and devotion belong to Him. Through His Holy Spirit, you continually give love to Him and one another. If someone should say to you, "I'd give you two million dollars for your spouse," or "I'd give everything I own for your faith in God," that wouldn't even tempt you. You wouldn't part with either, not at any price. But how much would you take for your job?

Besides your relationship with each other and God, your work needs to be something you truly love to do. Is it? Have you let scorn for additional training get in your way? Have you let a flood of applicants keep you from applying for the job you want? Have you tried to wash over a career preference in hopes you'll forget it exists?

If you're trying to let go of your "lost love" in the business world, you might succeed in holding it at bay or anchoring it for a time. You might engulf yourself with other concerns or splash through a daily deluge of work. But dreams don't drown easily.

In these first weeks of marriage, you and your partner might not be able to dive into another career. But you can buoy each other with your interest, encouragement, and prayers. So talk about what you want to do. Ask God to steer you toward the career He's planned for you—the one you can't help but love. Work toward goals together in God.

Prayer: Heavenly Father, we've been drifting in our jobs. Help us to know what You've given us to do and to receive from You all that's needed for this work in Jesus' name.

Journey with God: Many people change careers throughout their lives, but marriage begins a time for determining private dreams and mutual goals. List each. Ask God to show His order of priorities and the first step in His plan for each of you.

You have ravished my heart and given me courage, my sister, my (promised) bride; you have ravished my heart and given me courage with one look from your eyes, with one jewel of your necklace.
(Song of Solomon 4:9, AMP)

If your spouse feels led toward a drastic career change, you might need the eye of a jeweler. Instead of a finely polished, finished product, your husband or wife might seem like a gem in the rough. But look closely. Pray. Is something unexpected beginning to take shape?

What do you see? Can you catch a glimpse of the God-given talent your spouse needs to pursue this particular career? Can you adequately estimate the value of this dream? Can you see your faith and interest rising, enabling you to encourage your partner toward career fulfillment?

Encouragement comes as your spouse receives courage from the hopes, confidence, and belief you place in him or her. As newlyweds, you see the best in each other—well, most of the time. But can your husband or wife rely on you to keep on believing through potentially rough times and into a gem of a job? Are you willing to be ravished, to be carried away, by a heart for the jewelry God will fashion?

Someday your mate may tell you, "I couldn't have done this without you!" And yet it's not this person in whom you believe; it's God. It is He who brings dreams worth pursuing. It is He who gives the talent, interest, and ability needed. It is

He who gives the courage to go on. Therefore, it is God and His creative will you must treasure. As a necklace reveals its beauty and reminds you of its giver, so will God remind you of His presence and the opportunities He provides.

Prayer: Dear Heavenly Father, thank You for offering us Your dreams and giving us all we need to bring them into reality in Jesus' name.

Journey with God: As you bring your hopes to God in prayer, listen for His direction. In what ways does He want you to encourage each other toward fulfillment of His work in you?

[The Father] has delivered and drawn us to Himself out of the control and dominion of darkness and has transferred us into the kingdom of the Son of His love.
(Colossians 1:13, AMP)

As God fashions both of you, He might provide a new setting. Already your ongoing prayers and discussions have brought to light the dreams and goals you treasure. Now you might discover that, to pursue them, you need to attend school full time or accept a job transfer.

If you're the one whose career has begun to take shape, this can be an exciting, challenging time. But if you're the one making a temporary sacrifice, your home, friends, church, community involvements, and job might change—even though you'd rather everything stay the same. Yet you're willing to proceed, knowing the short-term situation contributes toward a long-term goal that's better for you both.

Because so much is changing, you can't help but feel a little scared. If you have to put your own career or wants on hold for a while, you might also feel a twinge of jealousy or a tinge of resentment. Maybe you feel depressed, angry, or sad, and that makes you even more upset—mostly with yourself for feeling this way! You don't want to say anything to your spouse because he or she might become discouraged, too, and what would that accomplish? But you keep recalling those old stories about people who gave up everything for a spouse's job or education, and when the stress ended they were dumped!

Into these dreary thoughts, God comes. He draws you away from your own reservations. He delivers you from fear, worry, anxiety, sorrow, and ill will. He gives *you* a job transfer —from wherever He finds you—into Christ's kingdom of love.

Prayer: Dear Heavenly Father, praise You for being with us in all places and in all things in Jesus' holy name.

Journey with God: List your concerns about any changes that affect you both. Discuss these with your spouse and pray about them together.

For we are what he has made us, created in Christ Jesus for good works, which God prepared beforehand to be our way of life.
(Ephesians 2:10, NRSV)

God has His work cut out for Him. When you agree to become who He sees you to be, He finds a way through obstructions. He removes anything that isn't diamond quality and fashions you into His shape and character so you can reflect His light.

God provides a unique setting for your work and lives. He knows you're not a solitaire diamond, so the living and working environment He provides will advance you both. A cut here, a beveled edge there, a nicely rounded corner, well-polished and refined. . . .

The trouble is, it can hurt to be faceted and polished. So say "Ouch!" if you like, and maybe God will not put so much pressure on you. But then He knows what you both can take. Perhaps His steady but firm hand reveals more faith in you than you have in yourselves.

You show what you're made of as unexpected circumstances or your spouse's needs reshape your plans. Your mettle and faith get tested as you reassure each other of a commitment and belief in a finished design that includes you both.

If you're the one with the heavy career responsibilities or hefty study load, you'll do what you can to keep this work from chiseling away private moments. You know that overtime, classwork, extensive travel, or after-hour activities can dull a romance, so you'll work to brighten your times together. Throughout your married life you'll continue to cut any excessive activities that obstruct your passion. You'll find a marriage fitting to you both because you're both made fit by God. You're all He continuously makes you, not two people set in stone, but changing and living for His work of you.

Prayer: Dear God, please help us to submit to Your shaping of us and our marriage in Jesus' name.

Journey with God: Does one of you have such a full schedule that the other feels bent out of shape? Talk with God and your spouse about ways you can keep these time losses from marring your honeymoon setting.

Until the day breathes and the shadows flee, I will hasten to the mountain of myrrh and the hill of frankincense.
(Song of Solomon 4:6, NRSV)

Do you have so much to do you can scarcely breathe? Do you feel as though you're running around all the time, trying to finish one chore after another? Do fears follow you like shadows—fears of failure, fears of debt, fears of somehow displeasing your spouse, a parent, an employer, or God?

If you wish you could just sit quietly on a mountaintop or have a long soak in a fragrantly scented bath—one that foams with hills of suds—do it. Take a walk along a beach and listen to the seagulls. Deeply breathe in the salty air. Or inhale the scent of pine needles, wet with rain. Watch cows grazing in a meadow and learn what you feel and see.

Do you see that some jobs aren't even yours? At work, you might not be able to change the list of tasks according to your preference. But around your home each chore can be distributed according to the available time or the level of energy and ability that God gave each of you.

It's more fun to work together in each other's company. Worries and chores soon flee. Cobwebs, clutter, dust, and shadows disappear. Laundry smells as sweet as frankincense—and so does your time together when you're finished. The yard and housework also get done without doing in either of you.

But if you find yourself alone with a mountain of work around your home, give yourself a breather. Turn on the radio or CD player and listen to hymns or something instrumental to your mental and spiritual well-being. Or put up your feet. Get your Bible and let your heart rest in the comfort of the Psalms. Instead of a frenetic pace, hasten to a mountaintop, indoors or out, where you can recall, Oh, look! God is here!

Prayer: Heavenly Father, we have so much to do and so little time to get everything done. Help us to take time out with You and each other in Christ's name.

Journey with God: Have you discussed the distribution of jobs around your house? These may change as necessity requires, but prayerfully consider which chores you're each to do.

Jesus replied, This is the work (service) that God asks of you: that you believe in the One Whom He has sent [that you cleave to, trust, rely on, and have faith in His Messenger.]
(John 6:29, AMP)

Depending on your background, you or your spouse may have heard people say, "I'm not doing that! It's a man's job!" Or, "Woman's work isn't for me!" But guess what? You *both* have the same job: Believe in the One whom God sent.

That's it! That's your full job description. It doesn't matter what sex you are and how much social or professional status you have. It doesn't matter if you possess impressive credentials, talent, ability, or money. It doesn't matter if you feel poor in time, energy, or interest. The job doesn't go away, and you're the only one who can do it anyhow. Only you can work out your belief—or doubt—in the One whom God sent.

As you arrange schedules and distribute jobs around your home, do so prayerfully and thoughtfully. Take each other's needs and routines into consideration as much as possible. Be willing to tackle new chores and generally do what's needed with cooperation and good humor. But don't forget the primary work to which you've both been called.

When duties mount faster than dirty dishes or the heel marks on linoleum, your faith might take a little elbow grease! You might wonder if weeds and doubts will always grow faster than you can keep them mowed. You might suspect there's always a furnace to clean, an air-conditioning filter to change, a garbage can to dump, a window to wash, or a floor to vacuum. The same person won't always do the same jobs. Some days it will be you; some days your spouse. But the same God will be served in both big or small chores as you help one another and put your faith to work in the ongoing message of Christ's love.

Prayer: Dear Lord, please help us to work well in Jesus' name!

Journey with God: List chores neither of you likes to do and pray about these. Get the message? The love of Christ puts you both to work. Have faith. *Believe* you're serving Him.

Sustain me with raisins,
refresh me with apples,
for I am sick with love.
(Song of Solomon 2:5, AMP)

Did you hear it on the grapevine? An apple a day may keep the doctor away, but Waldorf salad sustains newlyweds! If you're too lovesick to eat very much, just keep up your strength with small meals, fresh fruit, and vegetables.

If one of you likes to cook, great! But if neither has a flour-coated thumb, that could be even better. You don't need cooking ability to serve raw fruit and veggies. You just need clean, running water and a scrub brush. So instead of asking, "Who's turn is it to cook tonight?" just say, "Would you set the table, please? I'm washing dinner."

Nutritionists and Bible scholars agree that people need plenty of daily bread. This includes cereal from corn, oats, rye, barley, rice, and wheat. Also, dietitians recommend a small portion of meat or eggs each meal to provide ample protein. But don't sweat over a hot frying pan. Just pull out the broiler or grill, and slap on some saltwater fish, skinless chicken, or lean meat.

The best meal for you depends on personal taste and body type. But even with lettuce and tomato, you won't fare well on a consistent diet of hamburgers and fries. Greasy or not, they don't have enough vitamins, minerals, fiber, and complex carbohydrates to sustain you. However, with a side order of rye and walnuts in a Waldorf, dried grapes and fresh apples have what it takes to keep you food-grouped and going.

If you suspect you don't have adequate nutrients, add natural vitamins at mealtimes. Minimum daily requirements could be called minimal, but don't worry. God provides the *maximum*. He created a wonderful assortment of nutritional foods with varied taste, texture, and color to appeal to you and provide the sustenance your lovesick bodies really need.

Prayer: Dear Creator God, thank You for creating so many food choices for our good health. Help us to receive what You've provided in Jesus' name.

Journey with God: Are you finicky about food? List your favorites and ask God to show you what's missing from your diet.

____

____

____

____

____

____

____

____

And he took the seven loaves and the fishes, and gave thanks, and brake them, and gave to his disciples, and the disciples to the multitude. And they did all eat, and were filled.
(Matthew 15:36–37a, KJV)

Remember the Bible story about the loaves and fishes? Did you ever wonder what Jesus said when He gave thanks? Did He take the time to thank His Heavenly Father in advance for stretching such a very small amount to fill the needs of so many people? Did He thank God for providing *any* food in the middle of nowhere? Did He thank Him for forgiving everyone who came to dinner without first washing up? Did He thank Him that no one would get food poisoning? Did He thank Him for providing bread and fish instead of tofu?

No one knows exactly what Jesus said, but you can know this for sure: He thanked His Heavenly Father. He blessed the meal and those who ate simply because His thanks to God took care of the people as much as the miracle that followed.

If you're beginning to feel, "It'd take a miracle to get a decent meal in this house!" maybe you forgot to thank God—and the spouse who made *any* preparations. Or, if you've felt, "We just never seem to have enough to go around," maybe you need the grace to say grace.

You've already discovered your need to pray together regularly about every concern, but can you see the benefit of sitting down to meals together regularly, instead of eating alone and on the run? Can you see the nutritional value that "table talk" has in your marriage? Can you make a commitment to the blessed habit of gratefully sharing a meal and a mealtime prayer?

Prayer: Dear God, please remind us to say a blessing at each meal and to enjoy regular mealtimes together in the blessed company of Jesus' name.

Journey with God: Talk with God about your eating habits and thank Him for His good grace.

Tell me, O thou whom my soul loveth, where thou feedest, where thou makest thy flock to rest at noon: for why should I be as one that turneth aside by the flocks of thy companions?
(Song of Solomon 1:7, KJV)

"Let's do lunch."

People at work or school might ask you out for a quick bite, and occasionally that provides a nice break from your routine. But if it can be arranged, meeting your spouse for a midday meal provides a restful diversion to help you through the afternoon. The one you love can offer empathy, loving counsel, or a timely bit of advice about that big flock of worries or the little hassles you've had all morning.

If you attend school or work the day shift while your spouse works nights, you might have trouble finding a mealtime that suits you both. Sometimes you'll have to run an errand, take an exam, or attend a business meeting during your lunch hour. But as you arrange your schedules around each other's day, consider the spiritual, mental, and physical food value that lunching together brings: It gives you an opportunity to keep each other posted on the day's events. It gives you time to relax and laugh. It reminds you to keep each other in prayer.

Mealtime discussions over dinner can do the same—if you eat at home. But going out for dinner usually has its own separate menu. It costs more, takes more time, and ends with coffee and dessert or a sweet taste of romance. But during a busy day you're apt to eat lightly and just have fun.

High noon offers high hopes! All through the morning, you enjoy thoughts of seeing each other and having a change of pace. Maybe you'll only have time for a quick bite, but it comes with a warm embrace, a thankful prayer, and a delicious reminder of the one—and the One—whom your soul loves.

Prayer: Dear Lord, help us to taste Your love and laughter at mealtimes as we meet in Jesus' name.

Journey with God: Do you know each other's typical routines? Can you easily get in touch with one another? Do you keep mealtime appointments with God? Take note of your response.

____

____

____

____

____

____

____

____

____

He made its posts of silver,
its back of gold, its seat of purple;
its interior was inlaid with love.
(Song of Solomon 3:10, NRSV)

When you seek God about your work and lives, He does not toss aside what He's already put into place. Quite possibly, you both feel at peace about your home, education, and career choices. If so, maybe you've found time for hobbies.

Some you'll do together. Others will be solitary times. Still others won't appeal to both of you. But be aware that when one of you wants to do something and the other doesn't, a bored spouse can make a hobby of collecting hurt feelings.

Take, for instance, the classic example of a man and his car. Maybe he restores an old one, the first he ever drove. Or he lovingly waxes the metallic finish of a brand new model and babys the leather seats. Meanwhile, his wife feels left out. But right when she wonders if she's taken a backseat, her husband invites her to join him there. (Smart man!) So she does (smart woman!), and they enjoy the backseat together.

Whether your hobby has this happy ending depends on you and your spouse. Husband or wife, your mate might not want to interrupt your baking or woodworking or picture-painting or chariot-building. But that doesn't mean he or she wouldn't like to be invited to join you while you're doing something you love.

If you're involved in a pastime that doesn't include your spouse, the finished product may be praiseworthy or useful to you both. If not, talk about your hobby in an entertaining way, so your mate will enjoy hearing all about it. But don't expect to get applause from the sidelines. Pray about your exclusive time so you can make it inclusive as you draw your spouse's interest with good humor and God's love.

Prayer: Dear Father, help us to develop our own interests and add to our relationship without subtracting one another. Help us to give and receive Your spirit and love in Jesus' name.

Journey with God: List the hobbies you enjoy. Discuss and coordinate these with your spouse and God.

Behold, thou art fair, my beloved,
yea, pleasant: also our bed is green.
The beams of our house are cedar,
and our rafters of fir.
(Song of Solomon 1:16–17, KJV*)*

Remember when you first started dating each other? You took long walks on a beach or peer and watched the sunset over the water. You tried different sports, concerts, and restaurants. You went for a hike or a picnic in the woods. You raced across the park and swung high on a swing set, romping, laughing, and teasing each other playfully.

When you tired, you stretched yourselves out on a bed of thick, green grass. Above you, beams of cedar branched across the sky, and a leafy roof of fir or pine shielded you from the sun's glare but not its warmth. You listened to the symphony of a cardinal's call, a mockingbird's echo, the faint rustle of wind, the faraway sounds of children's laughter, a light patter of rain. Then. . . .

Then you got married and started exercising at the gym. You found a tape of bird calls, wind, and rain and kept it near the CD player to set a mood. You bought a firm mattress for your lower back and a nonaerosol can of environmentally correct pine spray.

While reminders of something you enjoyed can be pleasant, they are poor substitutes for being there. So pack a picnic! Get outdoors. Breath the fresh scents of sunshine and rain.

Enjoy a romp through the park or walk in the woods instead of a determined drill on muscle machines. Naturally, you'll get the exercise you need. But you will also keep yourselves—and your romance—from being on a treadmill. Look. Taste, touch, inhale, and listen. Explore the wonders of God's creation and the marvelous action of love.

Prayer: Dear Lord, forgive us for taking each other and Your creation for granted. Thank You for the beauty around us. What a wonderfully romantic setting. Help us always to enjoy it with praise to You in Jesus' name.

Journey with God: In the space below, note fun things you like to do together, indoors or out, and refer to the list as a reminder. Discuss and pray about these special times.

Now therefore ye are no more
strangers and foreigners,
but fellowcitizens with the saints,
and of the household of God.
(Ephesians 2:19, KJV)

During the first days of marriage, did you ever look at your spouse—for better or for worse—and wonder, "Who *are* you?" Sometimes you probably felt as though you didn't know one another at all, and in a way you didn't. You'd never before been each other's husband or wife.

Now that's changed. You're no longer strangers. You're starting to understand each other's likes and dislikes—well, part of the time. And you have reason to believe you will discover more about your mate as you go along.

As long as you *want* to find out, you will. God will help you. He's no foreigner to you, nor you to Him. You're citizens in His kingdom. You're family in His Household. You're His children. You're His saints.

Maybe you're thinking, "I'm no saint!" but God would not agree. It isn't that you're perfect, but in Christ you are perfected. Therefore, as you confess unsaintly traits to your Heavenly Father (and to your spouse as appropriate) you again become the person God knows you, in Christ, to be. You're neither strange to Him, nor a stranger.

So don't be strangers to each other. Give interest and attention to your spouse. Show your affection. Speak of your love. Seek fun things to share. When you can't do so without being totally strange to yourself, find a way to compromise.

Prayer won't compromise either of you. Together you'll learn God's ways. Sometimes they'll be completely foreign to your background or thinking. But because you trust God to be loving and impartial, you'll give Him the lead. You'll let Him bring you back together as His own saints—newlywed and newly reconciled to each other and to Him.

Prayer: Dear Father, help us to know and fully accept each other. Thank You for loving us as we are. Thank You for perfecting us in Jesus' name.

Journey with God: Has your spouse been acting strange? Ask God's help in talking about it. Use the space below to note insights or inspired ideas that come to your mind.

I was overjoyed when some of the friends arrived and testified to your faithfulness to the truth, namely how you walk in the truth.
(3 John 1:3, NRSV)

"I never get to see my friends anymore!"

If that's the truth, you'll probably be overjoyed when they arrive back in your life. If they go on and on about how married life agrees with you, your spouse might be glad too. But if they treat your husband or wife like a servant, pet, or wall fixture, your mate will be thrilled to see them go.

As you see the truth about your relationships, tread lightly. Since you love your spouse, you hope he or she will get along well with your friends, and they'll make a similar effort. But that doesn't always happen. Sometimes a spouse feels jealous. Sometimes an old friend does. Sometimes they simply have nothing in common—except you.

For your sake, they may try to be pleasant. They might even pretend. But for their sake and your own, prayerfully consider separate outings that don't conflict with your spouse's plans. If, for instance, your husband or wife has a noon business meeting, get together with your friends over lunch. Or while your spouse attends a ball game with former schoolmates, enjoy the company of an old chum.

This doesn't include a private meeting with a member of the opposite sex, of course, since misunderstandings or hurt feelings could occur. Nor does it mean going in opposite directions to show you still have a life outside of marriage. Just do what you can to keep your friendships in balance—and to stay in love. Walk in truth. Talk in truth. Let your love testify. And when you see your spouse again, show how very glad you are. Be overjoyed!

Prayer: Heavenly Father, help us to enjoy friendships with other people without taking away from our relationship. Help us to be truthful about what we want and need in Jesus' name.

Journey with God: Do you feel less than ecstatic about your spouse's choice of friends? Ask God to help you communicate your feelings without putting down anyone. Write down what God puts on your mind to say or do.

Marriage should be honored by all, and the marriage bed kept pure, for God will judge the adulterer and all the sexually immoral.
(Hebrews 13:4, NIV)

If your friends and spouse clash like mismatched wallpaper, ask God to give you insight into what's amiss. For instance, He may show you that your husband or wife has trouble accepting the fact that you have a life apart from marriage. Or perhaps you'll notice that your friend flirts or makes sarcastic remarks. In either case, your marriage isn't being honored—not by your friend or by your spouse.

Right away, your partner needs to understand that you're an individual. But you need to see that he or she doesn't want to be left out of your social life. If jealousies occur, you can acknowledge that troubling emotion and set it to rest by sensitivity, availability, and assurance of your love.

Meanwhile, your friends need to understand that you're now married. You're not the same single person they knew. You have a spouse with wants and needs entwined with your own. But your friends might also feel jealous and excluded. If so, acknowledge those feelings and let them rest in the assurance of your nonsexual love.

As you honor your own marriage, you act honorably. Your close friends, co-workers, parents, siblings, and others will see that you mean married business. For instance, they won't ask intimate questions if you keep your marriage bed pure and undefiled by not telling anyone about your sex life. They won't expect you to dishonor your spouse's confidence because they'll know you won't give away secrets. Real friends won't try to entice you from your husband or wife because they'll already have what they want—for you to be happily married. When *you* honor your marriage, you help to keep it that way.

Prayer: Heavenly Father, help us always to act honorably as we honor our marriage and You in Jesus' name.

Journey with God: Have you dishonored your marriage in some way? Pray for forgiveness—from God and your spouse. Then listen and note the responses you hear.

Let no evil talk come out of your mouths, but only what is useful for building up, as there is need, so that your words may give grace to those who hear.
(Ephesians 4:29, NRSV)

When you were growing up, a parent or teacher probably told you, "If you can't find something good to say, don't say anything!" Most of the time, that's sound advice, but, to build up your marriage, it's crucial!

Speaking well of your spouse to other people shows love, marital strength, and loyalty. Speaking well of your spouse to your spouse had better show what you think. Otherwise, he or she will have difficulty knowing when to believe you.

When spoken just for the sake of saying something good, compliments don't do any good. Untimely, untrue praise puffs a head with pride. Or if your spouse has discernment, false praise pricks his or her confidence and deflates what really is true. But starkly stating truths in an unloving, unkind manner won't help your relationship either.

For instance, maybe it really is true that you don't like your in-laws. But speaking ill of them won't build your marriage. Nor will you strengthen your relationship with your in-laws by saying what you don't mean. Phoniness or syrupy, flattering talk doesn't bond anyone. It just won't stick. But the truth told in love will hold you together strongly.

Spoken in love and kindness, truth builds relationships. So to say something truly good to your spouse and in-laws, find something good to say. You can. Look closely. Notice what's done well. Observe good values. Pray. Ask God to give you the right word to say at the right time to the right person in just the right way. Speak well of your marriage, your home, your church, your family. Speak well of your in-laws, and, if need be, ask your spouse to do the same.

Prayer: Dear Lord of our lives, please be Lord of our mouths in Jesus' name.

Journey with God: Have you said something that flatters or tears down? Repent. Wash your mouth with confession and an apology. Hear the upbuilding words God has given you to say.

Try to find out what is pleasing to the Lord.
(Ephesians 5:10, NRSV)

So what have you been saying lately about God? Does your personal life and marriage speak well for Him? Do you let what He says shape your thoughts, opinions, and beliefs? Do you say what He's given you to hear and speak?

During your growing-up years you heard what your parents thought and felt. If they're Christians who value God's word, they gave you a good heart- and headstart in your life and marriage. They gave you some idea of what God really thinks.

If so, praise God! If not, you may be hearing parental disapproval on all sorts of topics. "I don't know why you married such a stupid person!" Or, "Why are you always so mean to me?" Or, "You're just never any fun." Such talk tears you down and makes you doubt yourself, your spouse, and your God.

Most parents don't speak unkindly. Some just don't say anything good. They seem to have the mistaken idea that praise and appreciation will give you an inflated ego. If you or your spouse try very hard to please them, you might succeed, but you probably won't know it.

Or maybe the difficulty doesn't involve your parents at all. Maybe your in-laws, employer, instructor, or spouse make you feel you can't do anything right. If so, you're the one who has to do what's right by stopping such behavior. You're the one who has to make an important decision that affects your life: Will you stop trying to please anyone but God?

Praise God for letting you know what He wants. Thank Him for giving you instruction and encouragement in His word. Read what He says. Listen to His response as you pray. Don't wonder, "How can I please God?" Ask. Find out. He'll say.

Prayer: Heavenly Father, thank You for Your word to us in our prayer times and in the Bible. Thank You for Your Holy Spirit who lets us know what's pleasing to You in Jesus' name.

Journey with God: Who are you trying so hard to please? Ask God to speak to you about what pleases Him. Listen. Write down what you hear Him say.

Now this I affirm and insist on in the Lord: you must no longer live as the Gentiles live, in the futility of their minds.
(Ephesians 4:17, NRSV)

Do you and your spouse come from different backgrounds? Has your upbringing only brought up conflicting views? Does one of you have a foundation in Bible truths and Christian teachings while the other comes from fine people who don't happen to believe in God?

Nice people bring up such nice children. But apart from God, niceness alone doesn't provide the strength needed to hold up adults or keep them from toppling during a stout crisis. Those who think they're upright find out differently. Or they discover firm biblical ground hidden beneath them, set in place by a past generation who loved the Lord.

As a new family committed to God's truths, you stand for—and on—the provisions in His word. These give you godly understanding by which to build a marriage, make decisions, and influence others, including generations yet to come. So be sure you're building on sound, biblical principles—not your shaky backgrounds. That's ground behind you now anyway.

Although interesting and informative (sometimes shocking and amusing) your family histories are history—if you let them be. Instead of bringing up the past, bring in the Lord.

Let Him be Father, Mother, Teacher to the family you have now. Let Him give His parental guidance, counsel, and consent to the married life you're making. Don't listen to hollow words or futile thinking—not even from your own mind. Let God's word speak clearly to and for you as He helps your new family become upstanding and outstanding in Him.

Prayer: Holy Father, help us to lay aside the conflicts of our upbringing as You bring us Your word in Jesus' name.

Journey with God: What thoughts consistently trouble you? In prayer, bring faulty areas of upbringing and futile thinking to each other and the Lord.

Houses and wealth are inherited from parents, but a prudent wife is from the Lord.
(Proverbs 19:14, NIV)

"Every time you talk to your parents you get upset."

"What do you want me to do? I can't just walk away from them. I owe them everything."

You certainly do owe your parents a lot. Without them, you wouldn't be breathing. Without your mother, father, or parental caretaker to give you a home, food, clothes, medical care, education, and correction, your life wouldn't be as valuable to you now—assuming you made it this far.

So by all means, thank your parents often for their caring. Thank them for the time, love, and attention they gave you, even if you wished you had much more. Be grateful to them for the abuse or abandonment they *didn't* give. But if they handed that to you too, be grateful to God for His healing. You've inherited a lot from your parents, but you might want to throw away some of it. It's up to you to decide, "I don't like this thing they gave me." Then you can ask God to carry it into His forgiving love. He will. He knows what you've been given—good or bad. But He won't yank something from you until you're ready to let it go.

With love, thanks, and God's blessings, let go of your parents. Give them into the care of the Lord. Praise them often.

Thank them often. Look out for them often, but let God keep watch over you and your spouse—the person *He* provided for you to live out your married life.

Of course, you still feel an obligation to your parents and a deep regard. But above that, keep regarding your spouse —your new family—as God's priceless gift to you.

Prayer: God, bless our parents and all they've given us. God, bless both of us. We owe our love to You in Jesus' name.

Journey with God: Have your words or actions been swayed by how much you owe your parents? Pray for the discernment you need. Ask each other, "What do we owe God?"

Blessed be the God and Father of our Lord Jesus Christ, who hath blessed us with all spiritual blessings in heavenly places in Christ.
(Ephesians 1:3, KJV)

"Are you crazy? I don't owe my parents anything. Look at what they've done to me!"

Have you ever felt that you owe your parents nothing but hurt, resentment, anger, or at least a piece of your mind? If so, you owe them a lot. A lot of forgiveness and prayer.

Because you're seeking God's will for your lives, you owe yourself something too—the healing that's available to you in the name and power of Jesus. However, before you're able to receive this gift, you might need to give Him a piece of your mind—the pieces that cause the most pain. But don't worry. Christ can take it. He already has. He's taken your wounds to the cross and brought you back *His* peace of mind.

Will you take that? Will you accept the spiritual blessings awaiting you in Christ Jesus? Will you receive His healing love for yourself, your parents, or anyone in your life who has treated you unkindly or wounded you?

From the cross Christ forgave those who were, at that very moment, wounding Him. Can you imagine? Can you begin to comprehend the height or width or depth of His perfect, all-encompassing love? This love sinks into your deepest, darkest dwellings and lifts you into places most holy, most heavenly.

Christ's love enfolds and upholds the universe. Yet no matter how well you stretch yourself, you cannot reach very far without Him. You'll never be forgiving or forgiven by yourself. But with your *decision* to give and receive forgiveness in Jesus' name, you bring His power into each part of your life —past, present, or future. Through Christ, the Heavenly Father now places His heavenly blessings in you.

Prayer: Holy Father, it's so hard to forgive. Thank You that it's not a feeling, but a choice we make in the healing power of Jesus' name.

Journey with God: As God resurrected His Son from death on the cross for *your* sins, so will He resurrect your life in Him. First, He wants your confession and choice to forgive.

Wives, in the same way, accept the authority of your husband, so that, even if some of them do not obey the word, they may be won over without a word by their wives' conduct.
(1 Peter 3:1, NRSV)

If you've married an unbelieving spouse, you might be regretting that choice by now. You might be having trouble forgiving yourself for not seeking God's will before you exchanged your wedding vows. Now you just want to cancel the vows and exchange your partner—like an unsuitable wedding gift. Maybe you've even thought about shopping around for a Christian spouse before you buy into marriage again.

That's understandable. And you do have the authority to do this. But if you've observed God's work in your life, you know He can bring the bleakest situation into the healing light of His love. He possesses all the authority in heaven and earth. Yet He requests your loving conduct and consent.

God wants your spouse to believe in Him. Although He's perfectly capable of bringing this into being all by Himself, He'd much prefer your help. His word shows He anticipated this very situation, so He wants you to stick around. He would like for you to hold His light over your mate as He instructs and empowers you.

God wants you to join Him. He wants you to become His partner in marriage so He can become yours. This arrangement seems to be a more unlikely match than the one you've made, yet God asks you to be His spouse.

You have the authority to say yes or no. But, male or female, when you unite in the holy wedlock of Christ's name, you become a more powerful influence than you can pray for or imagine. You become God's love at work in your home and marriage—and in your spouse's life.

Prayer: Dear Holy Love, I praise Your strength. I marvel at Your power. Willingly, I give you the authority to work in me and my family in my married name of Christ.

Journey with God: Listen. What enlightening word has God given you about your behavior toward your spouse?

Likewise, ye husbands, dwell with them according to knowledge, giving honour unto the wife, as unto the weaker vessel, and as being heirs together of the grace of life; that your prayers be not hindered.

(1 Peter 3:7, KJV)

"A man's gotta do what a man's gotta do."

If you're a Christian wife, you might not be too sure about giving your husband the authority to do anything. You might not want to have an unbeliever speak for you or make decisions you don't like.

If you're a Christian husband, you might not see the need to believe an unbelieving wife about anything. You might not like her non-Christian attitude or perspective. You might think her wants, opinions, and values have no value.

In either case, as a Christian, you've gotta do what God says you've gotta do. Not only do you have personal knowledge of His saving power, you have acquaintance with His word, which says He wants you to be heirs together in Christ. But if your spouse doesn't believe in God—and you don't believe in your spouse—what trust is being shown in God's ability to effect the very change you want to see?

Because you believe in Christ, *you're* the one to believe on behalf of your husband or wife. *You're* the one who must turn to Him, in hope and prayer, to see His love and seek His grace and healing. *You're* the one who must treat your spouse with the love, care, empathy, affection, and attention that you want to be given and that this delicate situation needs.

Christian or not, as you treat your husband or wife with courteous regard, you show respect to God. As you honor your spouse's requests—not always with compliance, but with love and listening—your prayers will not be hindered.

Prayer: Heavenly Father, I thought You listened to me always. I didn't know I locked You out by shutting off my spouse—the very person for whom I pray. Forgive my hindrance. Help me to be open to Your grace and love in Jesus' name.

Journey with God: Do you need a prayer partner or do you need to pray for the one you have? Ask God to bring to your mind the prayers and partner with whom you're to pray.

When the woman saw that the fruit of the tree was good for food and pleasing to the eye, and also desirable for gaining wisdom, she took some and ate it. She also gave some to her husband, who was with her, and he ate it.

(Genesis 3:6, NIV)

Did you know that your husband or wife has a tremendous influence over you? Did you know you have the same? For good or ill, you both have the authority, power, and ability to sway each other by convincing and cajoling—or persuasively working to instigate godly change.

If you doubt that, look at Adam and Eve. Both knew God had provided their paradise. Both knew what He'd said they could and couldn't do. Both were right there—together—when temptation first appeared. And both could have said, "No!" But both got sneakily carried into sin.

Have you or your spouse let yourselves be carried away about something you once questioned? Did you pray about the matter, seeking God's will before moving in this direction? If not, one of you may have swayed the other into believing, "Hey, it's not so bad!" Or perhaps you allowed yourself to be fooled into accepting what you both wanted to believe.

Pointing fingers at each other won't help. Adam and Eve tried, and it didn't worked. So if you've now allowed sin to slither or slide into your honeymoon paradise, chase it out. With your confession and any restitution that's needed, you can do what Adam and Eve never did. You can *admit* your own choices and take responsibility for your actions. Then you can turn the matter over to Christ. Consequences might still come for a season, but as you choose forgiveness you pick the choice fruit of reconciliation. You take delight in the One who was there from the very beginning—the tree of life.

Prayer: Dear God, sometimes we want something so badly we can almost taste it. Help us to keep our lips sealed from ever sampling anything that's poisonous to our spirit, bodies, or minds. Thank You for sustaining us with the fruit of Your Holy Spirit in Jesus' name.

Journey with God: What fruit does God want you to pick?

Put away from you all bitterness and wrath and anger and wrangling and slander, together with all malice, and be kind to one another, tenderhearted, forgiving one another, as God in Christ has forgiven you.
(Ephesians 4:31–32, NRSV)

You've heard about the fruit of the Holy Spirit—love, joy, peace. So you probably know you can also pick fruit of an unholy nature. Although it won't win any prizes at the county fair, this fruit carries large seeds of bitterness that often show up in wrath and wrangling that lasts until someone finally spits out the truth.

Have you spewed your feelings, like bitter seeds, onto your spouse? Have you gotten into a contest, seeing who can spite the most? Have you, with malice, aimed directly for a vulnerable spot? Have you been so hurt or angry you just wanted to get even instead of forgiven?

What you spew is what you plant. So unless you want a marriage overgrown with hardheartedness, watch your rows! There's nothing wrong with having an argument or a dispute unless such rows take an unfair turn. But they won't if you keep the facts straight, your emotions even, and your heart soft enough to receive what your spouse is trying to say.

As you remove fruitless words from your tongue, you're better able to pray. No matter who's right or wrong, praying together helps you to be uprooted from doing things your way so you can be transplanted into God's way for you both. You might be really, really angry or really, really hurt and if so, that's really, really too bad. But don't let an unholy spirit take root in you. Exchange it for the fresh produce of God's own spirit—sown deeply within you by Christ.

Prayer: Heavenly Father, we don't want to go round and round in fruitless rows with each other. Help us to straighten our lives as we grow together in Christ's name.

Journey with God: Are you seeking God's will for yourself and your marriage, or are you growing contrary to Him? Does anything fruitless crop up in your disputes? Ask God to show you how to disagree productively.

Though I speak with the tongues
of men and of angels,
and have not charity,
I am become as sounding brass,
or a tinkling cymbal.
(1 Corinthians 13:1, KJV)

When you and your spouse disagree, you can be pretty proud of yourself. You've spoken like a true angel, haven't you? You didn't call each other names, right? You didn't use foul language or threats or hateful remarks, did you? You didn't put each other down or say anything so horrible that you regretted it later—correct? And yet you have this nagging feeling that you've been, well, uncharitable.

Maybe you just dislike arguing and wish you never had to disagree about anything. That could account for your feeling. However, it's unrealistic to expect perfect accord all the time—unless, of course, you and your spouse spend your lives holding the same note at precisely the same moment.

Or maybe you wonder if you've been uncharitable because arguing makes you feel you have a score to settle. That would keep you stuck on a single note too—unforgiveness—and that's not a loving tune. But if you feel there's something else at play during a disagreement, take the Bible's cue on the "sound of brass" and "tinkling cymbals."

In the middle of a debate, do you blow your own horn? In a heated discussion, do you add percussion? Do you chime in with high-pitched advice that's out of synch with either reality or your mate's mood? Do you scale a wide range of problems, creating a disconcerting strain on your relationship? Do you orchestrate a not-so-grand finale around yourself, drowning out your spouse? If so, the next time a disagreement gets off-key, play another tune. Instead of clashing or jangling, set the tone and tempo with prayer. Listen to the part you each play in God's symphony. Let Christ conduct you into an accompaniment of His harmonious love.

Prayer: Heavenly Father, forgive us for being out of tune with You. Help us to pray in our love of Jesus' name.

Journey with God: When you and your spouse disagree, what instrument do you play in disharmony?

____

____

____

____

____

____

____

____

____

____

Day 61

If I have the gift of prophecy and can fathom all mysteries and all knowledge, and if I have a faith that can move mountains, but have not love, I am nothing.
(1 Corinthians 13:2, NIV)

Do you know anyone who's a know-it-all? People like that make accurate predictions about something predictable. They solve unsolved mysteries, put together puzzling puzzles, and intellectually comprehend anything that's said. They're intensely knowledgeable and incredibly bright, but sometimes this seems like a glaring light that just hurts people's eyes—or feelings.

If you happen to be standing beside such a brilliant person in marriage, you probably feel dull-witted some of the time. As you live in his or her shadow, you might be tempted to put shades on your own knowledge or brightness. But don't! Your spouse married the person you are. He or she needs *you*—not to compare minds or flash wits, but to soften or screen the glare with your glow of love.

Maybe it's not that way, though. Maybe your spouse has dazzling faith that doesn't question anything. That seems great. And yet, when very real worries, fears, bills, or ills mount higher than the Himalayas, you don't feel comforted in hearing your spouse say, "No problem. God can take care of anything." You know that's true, but you really don't want to be told, "If you have enough faith, everything will be fine." Hearing this, you feel negated. Worse, you suspect that your spouse thinks problems only occur if you believe they do. It's as though your faith—or lack of it—is personally responsible for every dark speck on the sun!

Fortunately, God only requests tiny flecks of faith to move mountains. What's harder is consistently showing His love to your mate. Without love, a brilliant mind or dazzling faith means nothing. Oh, what a waste that would be.

Prayer: Dear Father, help us to receive Your love into our hearts, our minds, our faith, ourselves in Jesus' name.

Journey with God: Fill in the blank. "I am ______." Is this how your spouse sees you? Ask God who He says you are.

If I give all I possess to the poor and surrender my body to the flames, but have not love, I gain nothing.
(1 Corinthians 13:3, NIV)

In these first weeks as newlyweds, you've both been thinking about what you want to give and get out of marriage. Not only that, but you've considered what you want from your career, education, relationships, and church. If you've given thought to your new family budget, you've probably discussed the importance of presenting a tithe of your income to your church home as an offering to the Lord.

The Bible encourages generosity. As you give monetary gifts to your church or other ministries, you reach into the mission field. You help pastors, teachers, medical personnel, nutritionists, and other types of professionals profess their belief in Christ to those who desperately need His salvation.

Your monetary gifts also help the church where you've received an opportunity to worship God, have communion with His Body, and enjoy fellowship with other Christians. This financial assistance helps to provide your pastor's income, curriculum materials, musical aids, youth activities, church outreach programs, and monies for the upkeep of the building.

Besides these important works, your tithe works for you. As you place God before your finances, you know He'll honor your decision and obedience with His blessing. He will be in charge of your money and monetary needs. That's quite an asset. Yet all of these good gifts are not enough.

Even if you give everything you own to the church or the homeless people on the street . . . Even if you surrender your life's savings and give your time, energy, or talent entirely to the Lord . . . Even if you burn with zeal for God's work but do not love the people you help and the One whom you serve, you will gain nothing. You won't get anything out of giving without the priceless, generous, ongoing gift of your love.

Prayer: Dear Heavenly Father, help us to love You more than we can ever show in Jesus' holy name.

Journey with God: What do you want to get out of giving? Prayerfully consider what you've gained and lost.

Love is patient; love is kind;
love is not envious or
boastful or arrogant.
(1 Corinthians 13:4, NRSV)

"Would you please hurry up?"

Why? What's the rush? Does someone's life depend on your agile moves or accelerated pace? If so, quick! Call 911.

"I'm sick and tired of waiting around all the time! I told you when I'd be ready. Don't you ever pay attention to anything I say?" Apparently someone certainly does need to listen to a spouse's plans, but that person must be too sick and tired to hear well.

Love is patient—not an ill-mannered, ill-tempered patient who gets cranky if no one responds immediately to the call button. Love is kind—not "my kind" of tempo, but a love that keeps in step. This means one partner will often have to slow down to accommodate the other. But the slower mate will also pick up his or her feet instead of dragging them or stomping off in a huff.

In marriage, love does not arrogantly assume, "Hey, I have the only pace to consider!" It doesn't boast, "Listen, I'm doing this for you! I'm the one who's going places, so try to keep up, will you?" On behalf of a marriage partner, love often exerts effort, but not power or control.

However, love also doesn't envy a spouse who's on a fast, upwardly mobile track. It does not hold back a husband or wife from being the very person God created. Love doesn't whimper, whine, judge, condemn, or compete.

A struggle for dominance often arises in these first weeks, so be aware of your competition. And if you see any contention, stop right there and pray! Let your boasting be only in God and His love for you. Let His patience, kindness, and empathy win over you and your differences.

Prayer: Lord, we're no match for You. If we ask for patience, You'll test ours. If we pray to be kind, You'll bring unkind remarks or situations for us to handle. If we ask to be more loving, You'll bring people who aren't. Forgive us for even trying to compete with Your perfection. Help us to receive more and more of Your love in Jesus' name.

Journey with God: What hinders you from receiving God's love?

____

____

____

____

____

____

____

It is not rude, it is not self-seeking,
it is not easily angered,
it keeps no record of wrongs.
(1 Corinthians 13:5, NIV)

Remember that time you gave up what you wanted, just to please your spouse? Remember the time your husband or wife made a poor decision, but you came through with a creative solution that rescued both of you from disaster? Remember the time your spouse slammed the door so hard, a picture fell off the wall and you didn't say a word as you patiently cleaned up the glass and mess?

In Christ, you're a truly remarkable, wonderful person. So surely you don't want to be rude about what you remember now. To remind your spouse of awkward moments would be like displaying a photograph album that contains unflattering pictures of him or her but make you look perfectly wonderful all the time!

Love is not easily angered, nor is it easily angering. If you've revealed your handsome character at the expense of your spouse's appearance, you've at least tempted your mate to get annoyed. Or if you can easily recall anything your husband or wife ever did wrong, you're keeping count of no-account items. Turn in such books or records.

Instead of seeking ways to show yourself in a lovely light, show love for your spouse in light of God's acceptance and forgiveness. Keep track of the blessings and good gifts your husband or wife brings to you. Personally thank him or her and praise God. Isn't He great? Not only does God forgive your confessed sins and awkward moments, He totally forgets all about them. If you bring them up, He won't even know what you mean. That's not poor memory; that's love!

Prayer: Heavenly Father, we confess our wrongdoings and our wrongly kept accounts. Forgive us, Lord. Thank You for always forgetting our mistakes while remembering us in Jesus' name.

Journey with God: Do you keep wrongful accounts? Do you often call yourself, your mate, other people, or God to give an accounting? If so, confess and forget. In this space, recall what's right about each other and your relationship with God.

Day 65

Love does not delight in evil but rejoices with the truth.
(1 Corinthians 13:6, NIV)

"Told you so!" You've never said that, have you? But supposing you did, your spouse wouldn't appreciate the remark—especially if he or she already felt lousy about making a mistake or being wrong.

Ever since the first couple sinned, husbands and wives have been accusing one another. Or they blame themselves harshly again and again about what's wrong, and that just isn't right. It's not forgiving. It's not loving, and it often elevates one person above another.

If you just have to find out for yourself how to be right all of the time, here are some rules: Tiptoe lightly. Don't look down on those who won't accompany you in this performance. And (very important) find some kind of net to catch you when you finally fail to do the right thing.

Eventually you will. That's how this act always ends, and you can't change the inevitable conclusion. No one wants to see you fall, of course, so no one will be happy when you do—except, perhaps, an evil enemy. But your spouse and other people who love you won't even be able to watch.

If you're really, really good and keep your balance for a really, really long time, you might see it's lonely up on the high wire. Don't lower your morals or standards, of course. Just don't expect to attain them. But do consider this: What difference does it make if you're right?

What consequences, goals, or rewards do you hope will come when you joyfully prove your spouse wrong? Will that build a relationship? Will that build your ego for more than a half-second? Probably not. So don't focus on what's wrong with your spouse or yourself. Find out what's true. Don't be gleeful about being right, but rejoice about being in love!

Prayer: Dear God, help us not to be concerned about who's right or wrong. Help us to know how You want us to live in love with each other in our love of Jesus' name.

Journey with God: As you pray about a concern, ask for God's right answer, His truth. Ask, What's the *loving* thing to do?

Love bears up under anything and everything that comes, is ever ready to believe the best of every person, its hopes are fadeless under all circumstances and it endures everything [without weakening].

(1 Corinthians 13:7, AMP)

Are you feeling faint from arguing your position? Are you having trouble bearing up under the strain? Terrific! Now you can sit down. Relax. Have a nice cup of hot chocolate or chamomile tea with honey. Also, you might say something like, "Okay, I'm trying to listen. Would you please tell me again?" This could startle your spouse so much, he or she might sit down too and perhaps even speak more calmly.

As you begin to listen, keep your ears open for the facts. Try to hear the other side of the story—the one that's not at all like yours. If your spouse slips from a presentation of factual data, fine. Go with that—as long as you're not getting verbally abused and emotionally exhausted.

Often, your spouse's emotions can help you to understand a situation better. By encouraging your mate to talk about his or her feelings, you get beyond the point of logic, adding depth of emotion to the facts. So ask, "How did that make you feel?" Or, "Tell me what you're feeling right now."

Having you acknowledge his or her feelings or personal interpretation of facts will often be what your spouse wanted from you anyway. You may want the same. But neither will get what you've been missing unless you look and listen to each other's side of the story—the one your partner feels, sees, and believes. When you've both had your say, maybe you still won't understand. That's okay. You prayed for God's insight, and in time it will come. Until then, reassure each other of these ongoing truths: I love you. I like you. I need you. I believe in you—even when I just don't understand.

Prayer: Dear Heavenly Father, help us to believe more and more in each other, ourselves, and You in Jesus' name.

Journey with God: Do you believe God's word and promises in all circumstances, no matter how bad they seem? Do you truly believe in His love? Talk and pray about areas of disbelief.

Day 67

Love never ends. But as for prophecies, they will come to an end; as for tongues, they will cease; as for knowledge, it will come to an end.
(1 Corinthians 13:8, NRSV)

"But you promised!"

"I know. Things changed. I'm sorry. I should have just promised I would try." One of the hardest mistakes to face is the realization that everything would have been fine if it'd just stayed the same. Often people barely get one topic resolved and go onto another when they have to stop, go back, and reconsider. The only thing truly predictable is that, from one moment to the next, everything changes but God.

For better or for worse, it's a big mistake to think that nothing will ever be different in your lives than it is right now. If you like the way things are this very moment, that's how you want them to continue. (They won't.) But if you don't like the present situation, you'll be eager to hear about other options and alternatives. That's where factual data and statistics come in, bringing a little more light onto the subject —for now.

Only God's word has unchanging truth. However, knowledge and logical predictions can help you to see a situation better. If you stay open to ongoing possibilities, you'll see additional light slowly moving around the most shadowy topic. Eventually, those changing facts may help you to clearly see or better understand those things that don't change.

Someday predictions, prophecies, and promises won't be needed. You will have experienced the outcome, so you'll just know. Trends, factual data, and emotions will give way to God's eternal reality. Only His word will remain completely true. It will still express His love—the very love that's in you now. This love, God's love, true love will never end.

Prayer: Heavenly Father, everything we know and are can change tomorrow. That's scary, Lord. And yet we believe in Your unchanging love to see us through in Jesus' name.

Journey with God: Ask God to help you glimpse more of His eternal love. Remember His promises. Note here what you see.

When I was a child, I spoke like a child, I thought like a child, I reasoned like a child; when I became an adult, I put an end to childish ways.
(1 Corinthians 13:11, NRSV)

Aren't holidays fun? Won't they be twice as much fun in each other's company? They will if you prayerfully agree to make this a special occasion for you both.

Holidays have a way of changing adults back into children. Smells from the kitchen, favorite songs, old memories, and traditions come together for a season, and that's fun. That's exciting. But that's how it used to be.

This year is different. This year you have no special traditions in your home. Childhood games, songs, and favorite toys or foods belong to the past. You haven't lost what you once had. You've kept those memories. However, as this holiday approaches, you come with your hands free and ready to work at making new traditions together.

Some old favorites might be worth keeping. If so, think about what you treasure—songs, special foods, and activities you both can adapt to and enjoy. For example, if a highlight came from playing a particular game with siblings or cousins, you'll be disappointed if you don't get to play anything at all. However, if your spouse detests the game you wanted, you can compromise by finding one you both like to play.

Often holidays highlight your home, family, and the special attention you give one another. You try to pick just the right gift or menu. You make special plans. You do things for each other to show your love. But some things won't turn out as well as you'd hoped. When that happens, just put away childish expectations and disappointments as quickly as you can. Put away traditions you've outgrown. Put prayer into your preparations. Place God at the top of your gift list.

Prayer: Heavenly Father, thank You for bringing us into our first holiday season of marriage. Help us to offer our hopes, plans, activities, and gifts to You first in Jesus' name.

Journey with God: As you're making your holiday lists, check them twice—first with God and then each other.

And now these three remain: faith, hope and love. But the greatest of these is love.
(1 Corinthians 13:13, NIV)

"Happy Birthday to you!"

Did you have faith that your spouse would come through with a great present for your birthday? Did you hope to get something special, but didn't? Surprise! If you think you're disappointed, wait until you see your spouse's face when he or she realizes you don't like what you've been given.

"But I never said I wanted that!"

"I know, but I was trying to surprise you."

When someone says what they want and gets it, that's no big surprise. But when someone refuses to say anything and still hopes anyway, that's really surprising. Such odds can't help but come without a warranty.

Sometimes couples try to improve their chances at successful gift-giving by noting every item a spouse points out when they're shopping together. This too can prove surprising.

"But you loved this when you saw it in the store!"

"I know. But I didn't dream you'd buy it! It's much too expensive! For that kind of money, I'd rather have _______."

Surprised? Don't be. Out shopping, people often see things that remind them of something they liked or wanted as a child. Sometimes they respond enthusiastically to an item they think a relative or close friend might enjoy. Or they express wishful thinking and a whimsical, but changing, mood.

Before birthdays or holidays arise, let your spouse know what would be special to you. Don't hope the gifts will work out if you just have enough faith. Be truthful. Say what you like. Place your faith and hope in God and His good gifts—especially His always-surprising, guaranteed gift of love.

Prayer: Holy Father, thank You for giving us Your gift of new birth in Jesus' name.

Journey with God: Do you treat special occasions like candles on a cake, waiting for a big blow? What would make the day special to you? What gifts show love to God and your spouse?

Day 70

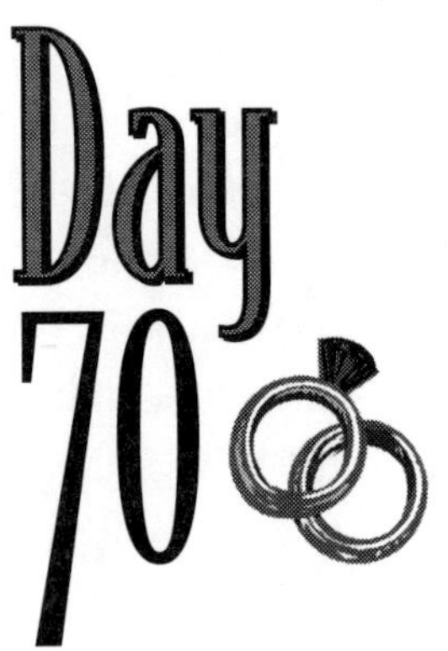

If then I do not grasp the meaning of what someone is saying, I am a foreigner to the speaker, and he is a foreigner to me.
(1 Corinthians 14:11, NIV)

Will an upcoming holiday or special event bring together both sides of your family? Is this the first time they've all been together, except, perhaps, at your wedding reception? Then you were probably too preoccupied to notice tensions among family members. But now you may feel emotions running higher than the voltage needed to power carnival lights.

Family get-togethers offer an amusement park for emotional whirls and strange exhibits of affection. With so many types of people mulling around, relatives often say things they don't really mean—or do mean, but didn't mean to say!

Most family performances only last a few hours, but that's plenty of time to get miffed or hurt feelings. There's also time for you and your spouse to wonder how many weirdoes you'll encounter. Then suddenly you seem strange to each other as you revert back to childhood roles. If, for example, you were known as the baby, the brain, the flake, "Mama's big boy," or "Daddy's little girl," you might start to play out that old part—as long as your relatives are around to watch.

Meanwhile, jovial responses, old jokes, corny remarks, fat kisses, and big hugs spin around you like a Ferris wheel! Into this carnival scene crowds another set of relatives with performances and expectations. Everyone talks at once. No one understands what anyone says, but everyone pretends they do. Differing backgrounds or expressions may make you wonder if you're talking to strangers too, and, in a way, you are. You can't always assume you hear what's really being said or see what's really going on until your spouse interprets. So speak for one another as the need arises, but translate each person and each moment with a familial view of love.

Prayer: Dear God, what a family circus! In Jesus' name, help us to show how Your love relates to our relatives.

Journey with God: Are you playing an outgrown part at family gatherings? Ask God to help you clarify misunderstandings and interpret His love. Write down what He brings to mind.

Jesus replied, If I have said anything wrong [if I have spoken abusively, if there was evil in what I said] tell what was wrong with it. But if I spoke rightly and properly, why do you strike Me?
(John 18:23, AMP)

Do both sides of your family speak rightly and properly to each other? Does anyone make improper gestures or remarks? Does anyone speak evil of you or wish you ill?

Too often, abuse comes through physical violence, mental injury, emotional affront, or spiritual attack. Each targets some part of your body, mind, or spirit and tries to harm, manipulate, or overpower your will, health, or inner self.

If you have received abusive treatment by someone's mouth or hand, by all means ask, "What did I do wrong?" Perhaps you've been terribly offensive and had such evil, cruel intentions, the person had no choice but to react against you. That's possible—but not probable.

Sadly, some Christians think Jesus set an example by just standing there and taking every kind of abuse on a regular basis. He didn't. He spoke not a word at His trial because His truth could not be heard in that place of conjured statements and outright lies. On other occasions, when people tried to harm Him, He slipped through the crowd and got away from their threats. He was in no hurry to die. He came to that moment only after agonizing sweat and blood. He came to that cross—one time—for one purpose only: To die for your sins and the sins of those who harm you now.

As you and your spouse adjust yourselves and your backgrounds to one another, relatives might offend you or vice versa. Such scenes are distressing, not abusive. However, if you're truly struck by abuse, don't just stand there! Ask why. Confront the person or situation with God's truth that you're given to say. Stand firm in your faith—not cowering, but believing.

Prayer: Dear God, forgive those who hurt the body, mind, and spirit You created. Thank You for giving Your healing word and truth in the redemptive action and power of Jesus' name.

Journey with God: Has God confronted you about harmful words or behavior? Discuss this prayerfully.

Indeed, there have to be
factions among you,
for only so will it become clear
who among you are genuine.
(1 Corinthians 11:19, NRSV)

Have you noticed how Christians who have been through a lot have sterling characters? Adversity tests their inherited traits or tendencies. Pressures remove the dross and purify whatever remains. In this way you can also expect a point of dissension to determine the strength, quality, and value of your marriage too. Such occasions help you to appraise your bonds of acceptance, forgiveness, and love.

If a weak spot begins to show in your relationship, you can count on its being tested. God may even allow stress or heavy burdens to bear down upon you—hard! Yet His word has made it clear that He wants nothing and no one to separate you from your spouse. So why does He seem to be doing that very job Himself?

In God, the two of you are one. He wants nothing to come between you—ever! He creates no dissension, no rifts. Nor does He want you to create them as you side with other relatives who agree with you when your spouse doesn't. However, if your marriage seems to be crumbling, God just might let it—long enough and far enough for you to want His love.

As His Holy Spirit comes into a rift, God draws both of you back together. He proves your commitment to each other and to Him. He tests your relationship from time to time so you can see how much you need Him with you. He reminds you that your love is genuine, enduring, priceless, and real.

So get real with each other. Be genuine in what you say and do. Be honest about your emotions, thoughts, facts, and feelings. As pressures bear down and fractures come, show appreciation of the sterling traits you see in your spouse. Express the high quality of your love.

Prayer: Dear Heavenly Father, help us to live in the purity of Your word and love in Jesus' name.

Journey with God: Has a falsehood or false action created a rift between you? Pray about this together. Talk about the unexpected realities of your married life.

Day 73

Let him kiss me with
the kisses of his mouth:
for thy love is better than wine.
(Song of Solomon 1:2, KJV)

"Hi, honey. I'm home."

When you and your spouse come home from work or school, do you greet each other with a kiss? Throughout the day or evening, do you acknowledge each other's presence?

In some marriages, people rush in the door, get into something comfortable, and fix themselves a drink to relieve the tensions of the day. When they finally notice their spouse, they say something like, "Oh, hi. Have you been home long?" Instead of receiving the benefits of a warm greeting, the other person might feel like a chilled leftover or a carbonated afterthought gone flat!

In your marriage one partner might be more outgoing and demonstrative while the other seems reserved or shy. However, both of you will soon look forward to an embrace at the end of the day. As you greet each other with affection, you hug away the tensions that have collected at work or school. With genuine interest, you brace each other further by asking, "How was your day?"

If something didn't go well, you can take time to talk about it before dinner. This keeps from ruining your meals (and digestion.) with unpleasant discussions and encourages you to exercise as you take a walk and talk about the day's events. If you forget to pray then about the present concern, you'll quickly remember when you say grace before your meal.

As you appreciate each other's comfort, encouragement, and prayers more and more, you won't take one another for granted. Regularly, your welcome will show affection as you hug, kiss, and remember to say, "I love you! I sure am glad to be home!"

Prayer: Heavenly Father, help us to demonstrate to one another our love in Jesus' name.

Journey with God: Have you withheld warmth or affection without realizing it? Prayerfully, discuss your methods of greeting one another. Ask your spouse, "What says 'I love you' to you?"

Day 74

By night on my bed I sought him whom my soul loveth: I sought him, but I found him not.
(Song of Solomon 3:1, KJV)

Guess what happens when an early bird and a night owl get married? They either catch each other coming and going, or they kiss a lot of sleep patterns good-bye! Sometimes the early bird awakens in the middle of the night and sees two big eyes, fixed open. Or the owl watches the bird getting droopier and droopier, earlier and earlier each evening. Both try to adapt so they can be together and get some sleep, but neither succeeds in becoming a night bird or an early owl.

If your sleep patterns conflict, you know the frustration of trying to find an agreeable solution. Or if one of you works days and rushes to classes each evening, you might find yourselves passing each other like ships in the night. So here's an option: Go to bed at the same time. Then go to sleep by yourself.

That's not as strange as it sounds. Say, for example, your mate needs to be in bed by ten o'clock, but you usually concentrate best on your work or studies around midnight. No problem. Get ready for bed. Read a portion of Scripture. Enjoy your regular devotional time together. Pray together, then say good night. Turn out the light, and then get up.

If your spouse dozes off quickly, you might want to lay still awhile and relax. Resting flat on your back for ten to fifteen minutes will help to ease the day's tensions. Then you'll feel somewhat rested and better able to spend a few hours working, reading, or studying until you're ready to go to sleep. Meanwhile, you've gotten ready for bed as a couple. You've turned in together. And you've ended the day in each other's close company as you embrace, pray, and say, "I love you. God bless you. Good night."

Prayer: Heavenly Father, thank You for being with us, day or night. Help us to take responsibility for our own sleep needs and find a serene solution as we rest in Jesus' name.

Journey with God: How do you feel when your mate goes to bed without saying good night? Discuss your sleep patterns and nightly farewells to each other and to God.

Day 75

(But weary from a day in the vineyards, I had already sought my rest) I had put off my garment —how could I (again) put it on? I had washed my feet— how could I (again) soil them?

(Song of Solomon 5:3, AMP)

"I'm so tired, I don't want to do anything but sleep."

If you're not getting enough rest, you probably won't be very good company with anyone, not even yourself. You'll find it's difficult to concentrate on your studies, or you'll drag through your work wearily. When you get home, you'll just want to put your feet up, nap on the sofa, or doze in a nice, warm bath—all of which will help you feel better but won't encourage intimacy with your spouse.

After a hectic day at work or school, you certainly need to rest and unwind, and so does your husband or wife. You both require adequate sleep and well-balanced meals to keep your energy levels from swinging up or down unevenly. If you still lived alone, you'd probably just eat and sleep whenever you felt like it, and no one would care.

Since you're not by yourself, it may take awhile to adjust your schedules, but you'll enjoy each other's company during meals, rest, and leisure. However, if you often seem tired or disinterested in food or play when you're together, your partner will begin to wonder what's wrong.

"I told you! Nothing's the matter. I'm just tired."

If you say that every week, consider why. Are you trying to accomplish too much in too short a time? Are you allowing less sleep than your body requires? Are you filling up on snacks that offer too little nutrition to keep your body healthy? Are you fretting about a problem that you need to discuss with your mate and God?

If you're not feeling great, don't try to hide it. But investigate what's wrong. Stay awake to the possibilities. Discover what makes you tired. Prayerfully, make changes as needed. Do what you can to bring ongoing energy and interest to your married life.

Prayer: Dear God, please level our paths in Jesus' name.

Journey with God: What keeps you from resting or eating well?

I opened to my beloved; but my beloved had withdrawn himself, and was gone: my soul failed when he spake: I sought him, but I could not find him; I called him, but he gave me no answer.
(Song of Solomon 5:6, KJV)

"Not tonight, honey. I have a headache."

Do you expect your spouse to be available whenever it suits you? Do you have that same standard for yourself? Accessibility to one another doesn't involve lovemaking only but includes being ready to listen when your husband or wife needs to talk. If you've had a difficult day yourself, you might not be too eager to hear about more problems. And yet, unless you remain open to discussion, you can't really expect your spouse to show very much interest when you'd like someone to listen to you.

"Being there" for one another means giving an immediate response. This doesn't mean you're forced to participate, actively, right then in a conversation (or sex), but your spouse does need your prompt reply. He or she needs to know (1) if you've heard the request, (2) if you care about what you have heard, and (3) if you prefer another time.

Delays don't *have* to be a put off. But putting off your spouse does occur if you ignore or forget what's said. Then your mate must decide whether to bring up a topic again (at the risk of being a pest) or to pretend something doesn't matter when it does. This may be more convenient for you now but won't make a close relationship accessible to you later.

Closeness doesn't come from distancing yourselves from each other. Maybe you really do have a headache. Maybe you really are distracted or tired. But with God's help and clear communication about each other's wants and needs, you close the gap. Together you can choose to pray, acknowledge one another, and make available time expressive of your love.

Prayer: Holy Father, thank You for always answering us—yes or no—in Your loving response to our needs in Jesus' name.

Journey with God: Everyone has some way of withdrawing. What, where, when, why, or how do you try to hide from your spouse? From yourself? From God?

(Please) do not look at me,
(she said, for) I am swarthy.
(I have worked out) in the sun and
it has left its mark upon me.
My stepbrothers were angry with me,
and they made me keeper of the
vineyards; but my own vineyard
(my complexion) I have not kept.
(Song of Solomon 1:6, AMP)

"Marriage certainly does agree with you!" Translated, that often means, "You look happy, but haven't you gained ten pounds?" Maybe you've lost weight. Either way, do you feel better? Do you feel good about yourself?

Not long after the wedding, some people start to think, "I'm married now. Who cares how I look?" Your spouse does, and you probably do too. However, the emphasis has changed. You're not trying to attract a mate. You've done that. Male or female, you're now trying to keep attracting the mate you already have.

Taking care of your appearance shows you care about yourself and the spouse who wants a lifelong look at you. That doesn't mean expecting each other to go around in full makeup or formal business attire. What you have on (or off) doesn't matter nearly as much as the energy or healthful glow you bring to each other and your relationship. After awhile, neglecting yourself will leave its mark—on both of you.

If you've been letting yourself go, hurry! Get yourself back! Enhance your appearance with appropriate apparel for your size, shape, and coloring. Find out what your spouse thinks of various styles and how they suit you. Go shopping together. Express your personality in what you choose to wear, but don't wear yourself out trying to look glamorous. Be yourself. Establish healthy, well-balanced habits for your meals, rest, and play to keep in shape and attractive to your spouse. You'll feel better too. With care and prayer, you'll tend your own skin and everything wrapped inside.

Prayer: Heavenly Father, forgive us for not always taking care of ourselves. Help us to show proper respect for the bodies, minds, and spirit You created in Christ's name.

Journey with God: How well do you treat your spouse's body and your own? Ask God to give you His impression of anything you're to do differently.

Come, my beloved,
let us go forth into the field;
let us lodge in the villages.
(Song of Solomon 7:11, KJV)

Do you know what very old people and very young people have in common? They both know what's fun. Since you're probably somewhere in the middle of those age groups, you may need to remind yourself to have a good time. To your husband or wife, you might need to say, "Yo, beloved! Come play." Or, "Hey, honey, let's spend the night in a motel."

If you live in the city, a weekend in the country offers a break in perspective and routine. If you're country folk or reside in a small town, you might enjoy the wonder of city lights strewn like stardust across an evening sky.

Besides a change of setting for the weekend, look for a change of pace. If, for instance, you spend hours commuting to and from work, then racing around once you get there, you might welcome an evening's entertainment at a theater where you can sit down and relax. If you have sedentary jobs, you might prefer to stretch yourself with a game of volleyball, tennis, miniature golf, or a hike near peaking waves or peaking mountains.

The idea is to get out of your normal workweek and into an outing that fits both of you reasonably well. A total change of pace and setting provides interest and renews enthusiasm for your homecoming. That's assuming, of course, that all is well. If not, you may be able to see what's bothering you at home or work after you've been away. Feeling refreshed by your outing, you will have a better idea of what you're supposed to do. A temporary change of surroundings can help you to know what to change around you, permanently. But, home or away, be sure to lodge in the community of prayer.

Prayer: Heavenly Father, help us to know what changes to make in our routines, temporarily and permanently. Please show us the fun-loving times You've created for us in Jesus' name.

Journey with God: When you go away for the weekend, do you take a Bible along? Ask God where He'd like to accompany you on your next outing.

May Christ through your faith [actually] dwell (settle down, abide, make His permanent home) in your hearts! May you be rooted deeply in love and founded securely on love.
(Ephesians 3:17, AMP)

"Has our kitchen always been this small, or am I just now noticing it?"

One of the dangers of leaving home is coming back to dissatisfaction. After eating in a fine restaurant, you might notice you're not getting such gourmet results with tinny, inexpensive cookware. After bathing in a whirlpool at a resort, you might shake your head (or a lot of cleanser) over the condition of your tub's enamel. After visiting a friend or relative in a spacious home or terrific locale, you might wonder when your own place started looking so tiny, terrible, or trashy.

What other people and other places have won't bother you at all if you like where you are. But if you wish that one little thing could be different, you'll probably notice that immediately. That's fine, if you can do something about it. If not, just settle down.

In your own hearts and minds, settle on the style and size of dream house you prefer. Settle on a location, neighborhood, and budget you can afford or easily work toward together. Settle on specific conveniences or necessities you would most like in a home. Until that's available, settle down in deep appreciation of all you have.

In this place or another, let your security system and marital foundation be built in Christ's love. Let God provide His heavenly places where you can live peacefully now and—happily—ever after.

Prayer: Heavenly Father, sometimes we don't even know what we want. When we do, it's hard to wait. Help our faith to settle down deep into Your love. Help us always to make room for You so that You're our home and we're Yours, now and forever, in Jesus' name.

Journey with God: In the space below, note what you'd like in a home. Listen. How does God want to be at home with you?

Did not one God make her? Both flesh and spirit are his. And what does the one God desire? Godly offspring. So look to yourselves, and do not let anyone be faithless to the wife of his youth. For I hate divorce, says the Lord.
(Malachi 2:15–16a, NRSV)

In your first weeks of marriage, you've made all sorts of adjustments in your routines, hopes, and expectations. You've experienced the give-and-take relationship that comes with married love. You've discovered aspects of faithfulness you didn't even know existed a few months ago. And now you have proven your loyalty to each other as you faithfully continue to pray together, seek God's word, and learn more about Him—and yourselves—in this devotional time.

If, however, you've consistently been holding out for your own way, you're now headed for divorce. Sorry, but it's the final destination for that direction. Personally, God hates that route. But it's your choice: You can head in separate ways that take you farther and farther from each other. Or you can head toward God's hope, God's expectation, God's destination, and God's desire for you: His Headship in Christ. Whether you're near or far, no one else can bring you close together. Some may think a child will reestablish their relationship, and that's true in some ways. Having a baby will indeed keep you legally, morally, logistically, and emotionally attached to one another as long as you three shall live. But this won't help your marriage or your child.

God alone can make you one in Him—one body, one mind, one spirit. As you seek His direction for you, this may bring children too. That's up to you and God. But with or without a baby, union in Christ makes you God's own child. You're His godly offspring. His Holy Spirit continues to produce and develop fiber and muscle in you and your married life.

Prayer: Dear Father, forgive us for going our separate ways, apart from You and each other. Bring us close together in the blessed union of Jesus' name.

Journey with God: Prayerfully talk about having children. Prayerfully talk about being God's child in His spirit.

That is, that we may be mutually strengthened and encouraged and comforted by each other's faith, both yours and mine.
(Romans 1:12, AMP)

Do you really want a baby? Have you tried, but so far nothing's happened? Have you had the disappointment or grief of a miscarriage? Did you have an abortion before realizing your own value as God's offspring? Do you wonder if you've been forgiven? Will you forgive yourself and your spouse?

In Christ you can. His peace will then be with you as you accept His forgiveness and the healing power of His love. He will provide all the encouragement, comfort, strength, and upbringing that you need.

At various times in your marriage, you'll enter an area of hardship, but don't stay there. Go through it. With each other's forgiveness, love, and prayers, you're better able to move on. But God Himself provides the power for you to pass through anything you encounter. He is your Passover—from hurt or grief or disappointment—into a fruitful life in Christ.

In Christ you are forgiven. In Him your lives become productive and blessed. Perhaps you'll have the additional blessing of children, but this does not determine your mutual affection or God's. As His family you will continue to grow in your acceptance of who you are—one family in Him.

Should you discover a baby will soon join you, praise God! This might not seem like the best time, but it will be in God's time. He knows what you can handle, and He knows to Whom you will turn. He stands by you in faith: your faith in Him and His in you. Therefore, you have His courage, His strength, His comfort to build His family of you in the Lord.

Prayer: Heavenly Father, sometimes we think we want children. Sometimes we're sure we don't. We have little faith in our own timing or knowledge, but we have confidence in You. Thank You for healing, guiding, and strengthening us in the power and purpose of Christ's name.

Journey with God: Do you feel weakened, sad, or discouraged about a past choice or direction? Do you believe God has the power to forgive and restore? Talk about this with Him.

Who shall separate us from the love of Christ? shall tribulation, or distress, or persecution, or famine, or nakedness, or peril, or sword?
(Romans 8:35, KJV)

Are you ready for a nonsporting event that's always in season? In marriage, the scoreboard doesn't look promising! You'll encounter scary statistics that show no one is exempt. Everyone is fair game. So, just like other couples, you can find excuses to separate or call off the whole match.

Some crowds will cheer you onto a divorce court. Those who miss your company at a singles match might like to see you rejoin their team. Or a team at work or school might want you to be more available to them and their goals. A pack of adoring fans, an old flame waiting in the stands, or a worldly crowd might hope your marriage will end.

Do you want a record of defeat? You needn't have one. In Christ, you're more than conquerors. You have already won His love. Nothing and no one can separate you from that—except, of course, yourselves by your own choice.

If marriage has already separated you from your job, education, home, hopes, parental approval, peer approval, or anything else, you might be tempted to give it up. If you have an unbelieving spouse who isn't a team player, maybe you won't even have a choice if that person decides to walk away. But if you and your spouse choose Christ's Holy Spirit to coax and lead you, nothing in heaven or on earth will stop Him from doing just that.

Temptation, trial, and torture did not keep Christ from attaining your salvation. Adversity, anguish, and affliction did not stop Him. Although bruised, thirsty, and naked, He still headed for the cross. He died. And even in His death, His enemies pierced His side. For a while, He seemed to be defeated. Yet tribulation, distress, persecution, famine, nakedness, peril, and sword did not hold Him captive. From death, He arose! Now, despite the odds against marriage, Jesus Christ carries the power you'll always need to win.

Prayer: Lord, resurrect us in the power of Jesus' name.

Journey with God: What needs saving in your marriage?

We are assured and know that [God being a partner in their labor] all things work together and are [fitting into a plan] for good to and for those who love God and are called according to [His] design and purpose.

(Romans 8:28, AMP*)*

"We really love each other! But we're driving each other nuts! What do we do?" Simple. Stop driving.

Remember how these first weeks of marriage often involve a power play? It's not that you want to lord a position of authority over your spouse. (Well, maybe, sometimes.) But most of the time most people don't want to lose themselves in someone else's backseat. Chances are, you'd prefer to keep your seatbelt up front too.

As Christians, you might be willing to leave the driving to God, but you probably aren't always sure what that means. Does He, for instance, want you to let Him bus you to this or that destination without giving you a say in where you go or what you do with your own lives? No!

If God had wanted you to be creatures under His power without any choices, you wouldn't be married. You would be teddy bears. Since you're not stuffed animals, you aren't expected to stuff your thoughts, feelings, wants, needs, or mistakes. You're to bring those to God in prayer. Listen to His word. Obey. And do what He gave you a right to do—choose. He hopes you'll choose Him. God is love. So He wants you to benefit from His love. But He also wants you to love Him—something teddy-bear passengers just cannot do.

As you get to know and love God for who He is, you realize He knows and loves you more than you do yourselves. He better understands your situation and destination. So you can trust Him to fit everything—even disappointments and mistakes—into a working plan with adjustable seats, custom-designed for you. He doesn't want you *under* power but *in* His. Trust God to be the driving force in your married life.

Prayer: Dear God, sometimes we're not sure where You want to take us. But we choose to trust Your driving ability and Your perfect record in Christ's name.

Journey with God: Has something in your marriage taken a wrong turn? Ask God how to straighten the wheel.

Day 84

Likewise the Spirit helps us in our weakness; for we do not know how to pray as we ought, but that very Spirit intercedes with sighs too deep for words.
(Romans 8:26, NRSV)

"Families who pray together stay together."

Overwhelming statistics prove the wondrous truth of that old adage. Yet despite the familiar saying, most couples don't even think about praying together. It doesn't occur to them to bring their concerns to God throughout the day or to close each evening with a prayer time. Some feel too awkward or foolish to try. But most just wouldn't know how to pray with a spouse.

You do. You've seen that prayer transforms attitudes, changes situations, and blesses those who pray. For instance, if you and your spouse disagree or cannot understand each other's point of view, you know it's time to stop arguing and start praying. You'll barely say, "Let's pray about this right now," before you'll have the insight needed.

Sometimes, though, you won't have any idea what God intends. During those times, ask Him to give you His prayers to pray. Then expect Him to grant you His thoughts on what you're to do. Trust Him to bring you His impressions of how you're to pray as you ought.

You ought to find plenty of Bible prayers and promises to claim as your own. As you get to know God's word better, you'll find these passages give you immediate passage into His will. These, too, are God's prayers to pray.

The best-known example, of course, is Christ's pattern. When His disciples realized that Jesus received extraordinary power from His talks with the Heavenly Father, they asked, "Lord, teach us to pray." He did. Now you have the Lord's Prayer as the Lord's answer to *your* prayer: "Oh, please tell us! How do we pray about this?"

Prayer: Dear Father, thank You for teaching us to pray powerfully in the word and holy spirit of Christ's name.

Journey with God: Using the Lord's Prayer or Our Father as a guide, begin to pray each day with the personal adaptations God brings to your mind.

Pray, therefore, like this:
Our Father Who is in heaven,
hallowed (kept holy)
be your name.
(Matthew 6:9, AMP)

Did you know the Lord's Prayer or Our Father comes with a warning attached? Before Jesus gave His pattern of prayer to those who sought His example, He issued some statements of caution. In so doing, He confirmed what the disciples already suspected: Prayer is powerful stuff! Therefore, Jesus showed His followers (including you) how to handle prayer with proper care and respect.

In the sixth chapter of Matthew's Gospel, Jesus gave these cautionary principles: Don't be hypocritical when you pray. Keep your prayers private, not for show. Don't chant a phrase like a mantra, nor use puffy words to sound good to yourself or impress other people. But do be aware that God hears your prayers even before you speak.

The idea is to address your prayers to God alone—not to yourselves or other people. Let your praise, petitions, and thanksgiving express what you really mean—not what you think you're supposed to say to show off your religious fervor or piety. Let your prayers bring your pure and genuine interests to God, who is Himself pure, genuine, and holy.

Before you even say a word, Christ instructs you to pray in keeping with God's holiness. And yet He does not offer these instructions to help you manipulate or successfully approach an unreachable, distant, apathetic deity. No, He begins His prayer—your prayer—by speaking to Our Father in Heaven. Through Christ's life, death, and resurrection comes your *only* prayer for His Heavenly Father to be your Heavenly Father too. Praise Him. Show reverence to His name.

Prayer: Dear Heavenly Father, we praise You for bringing Your holy name into our marriage. Help us always to honor You with our words, thoughts, and prayers. Praise You for showing us the whole truth of Your pure love for us in Jesus' name.

Journey with God: What needs do you think God sees before you even ask? Offer these to Him with thanksgiving.

Thy kingdom come. Thy will be done in earth, as it is in heaven.
(Matthew 6:10, KJV)

Stop right there! Until you know what you're getting yourselves into, maybe you'd better not pray any further.

As Jesus cautioned in Scripture, you need to count the cost before you start to build. Similarly, building a prayer life—or upbuilding your marriage in prayer—requires payment. You have to exchange your will for God's.

If, for instance, you want to build or buy your own home, you first have to sign all sorts of documents, clarify your expectations, authorize inspections, approve changes, and finalize the agreement. Unless you have large quantities of cash, you'll also need a loan approval. Then, to get one, you'll put your word, will, promise, and name on the line.

That's what Jesus does with your prayers. He gives you power that you don't have but need to upbuild your faith and lives. He won't endorse anything displeasing to God nor will He grant His power and authority to every whim or wish you'd like to see included. But if your homebuilding plans agree with God's will, word, and ways, Christ will take your prayers to His Heavenly Father. He'll even sign necessary documents, on your behalf, with His blood.

Praying in the name of Jesus brings your prayers to God, using the credit established by His Son. You're encouraged, of course, to talk to God about anything you want. But you're not advised to pray for Him to grant even a tiny request that goes against His will. It's not that God can't or won't allow such favors. No, the problem is, He might! And then where would you be? You'd be stuck in what you willed or what you wanted rather than in the blessing God knows is blessed.

When you're ready to see what He's prepared for you (and to trust Him even if you don't see), *then* you're ready to ask God's kingdom to come and His will to be done in your home, your family, and your marriage. So go ahead. Pray with confidence. To your every prayer, sign Jesus' name.

Prayer: Dear Lord, help us to live in Jesus' will.

Journey with God: How does God want His kingdom further advanced in your marriage? Listen to His prayer for you.

Give us this day our daily bread.
(Matthew 6:11, KJV)

How's your budget coming? Have you decided who will be responsible for balancing the checkbook and paying the bills? Have you agreed on each item and remembered to include the average costs each month for groceries, rent or mortgage payments, clothing, transportation, insurance, utilities, phone, cable, fax, or taxes? Do you have a daily allowance for lunch and coffee breaks? Do you still have enough cash for tolls, carpools, or parking? If not, do you feel annoyed with yourself or with your spouse?

If your daily needs aren't being met, you won't have to look far to find someone to blame. You'll be able to point to an employer who forgot about the raise you'd been promised. Then there's the landlord, the realtor, the insurance agent, or the utility company who will eventually notify you of a price increase. Meanwhile, the costs of groceries, long distance, cable, and, of course, taxes will go so high, you'll get a crick in your budget trying to stretch your income. And if you cannot possibly get what you want, you can always blame the government—or the spouse who's paying the bills.

Some people blame God. They want to know why He doesn't supply their daily needs easier or quicker. They demand an explanation, an accounting of Him—neglecting, perhaps, to look at their own mismanagement of what He's already given. They complain, but do they pray? Do they ask for anything?

If you've done what you can to be good stewards of the time, talents, and money God has provided, maybe He's waiting for you to request more. Until you ask, "Father, would You please give us all we need today," how will you be sure He's the One who produces everything you have and everything you want? How will you know He can afford you? How will you receive the daily allowance He generously provides?

Prayer: Dear Father, forgive us for blaming and complaining. Help us to recognize You as our provider in Jesus' name.

Journey with God: Have you budgeted each day to include Bible reading, devotions, and prayer? As you look to God for your daily allowance, allow Him your day.

And forgive us our debts,
as we also have forgiven
(left, remitted, and let go of the debts,
and have given up resentment
against) our debtors.
(Matthew 6:12, AMP)

Oops! Payback time! What do you owe—a promise, a pledge, a vow, a bill? God's word clearly states that He wants you to be indebted to no one but Him. Otherwise, a person might try to oversee your lives and finances. You might have no choice but to defer to them and their wishes—especially if they lord themselves or your promise over you.

But maybe this doesn't concern money. Maybe a parent, older brother or sister, teacher, employer, or other authoritarian acts as though you owe a lot. If anyone thinks that unfairly, can you repay them with your forgiveness? Can you give them at least a tiny measure of the pardon God has given you?

You don't need to pardon people with excuses for them or their behavior. You don't have to find an explanation or logical reason for their words, attitudes, or actions. Even if you feel kindly toward those who want you to pay up, you wouldn't be offering them your forgiveness but your verdict of the person or situation. "She just can't help herself." Or, "He didn't know what he was doing." That's judgment. And that's up to Christ to decide.

From the cross, Jesus did indeed say, "Father, forgive them. They know not what they do." As He came to pain and death, that was His evaluation, His verdict, His judgment. At an excruciating cost to Himself, Christ judged everyone. And He forgave. How much will it cost you to do the same? Isn't it payback time of *everything* you owe Christ to forgive?

Prayer: Dear Lord, forgive us for our unforgiving spirit that trespasses against Your will! Help us to let go of every old debt stored up in anger, hurt, resentment, or pride. Release us to receive more of Your forgiving love for ourselves and others in Christ's name.

Journey with God: To whom or what are you indebted? Ask God to show you how to let go of what's due you so you're free to accept and hand out Christ's forgiving love.

And lead us not into temptation,
but deliver us from evil.
(Matthew 6:13a, KJV)

"Yes, Lord. Deliver us from evil." That part clearly makes sense. But doesn't it seem strange to you that Jesus included in His prayer pattern the request, "Lord, lead us not into temptation."

The Bible states that God does not *tempt* anyone. And yet Jesus' unusual request implies that God just might lead you into temptation. Why? Why would a loving, forgiving, caring, merciful God do such a thing? Could it be because you asked? Could it be that your prayers apart from God's will have indeed lead you into temptation if they're answered with a divine yes?

In other words, if you ask for something against God's will, He may let you go ahead long enough or far enough to see, "Oh, no, Lord! I made a mistake! I don't want this after all."

Christ said what He meant to say, because, like you, He had been tempted. After His baptism, the Holy Spirit led Him into the wilderness where He was tempted with His possibilities, not God's purpose. If He wanted, He could use His power for personal or political gain. If He wanted, He could avoid the cross. He could end it all right then, fast, by jumping from a cliff. Christ could have spared Himself suffering, yet He would have lost His resurrection power, and you would have been lost for all eternity in sin.

The same Christ who did not give in to His temptation, prays now that you'll not give in to yours. He has the power to deliver you from evil. He has the long-suffering love to see you through anything you face.

Prayer: Dear Lord, praise You for delivering us from every evil thought, word, or deed that we have done. Praise you for delivering us from the evil powers that tempted You. Help us to know, pray for, and follow Your will in Jesus' name.

Journey with God: What do you feel tempted to do? Do you need to be delivered from a spiritual influence that's not of God? Pray for Christ's power to overcome.

For thine is the kingdom,
and the power,
and the glory, for ever, Amen.
(Matthew 6:13b, KJV*)*

"What a wonderful couple you are! You're so blessed."

Yes, you are. When you choose the kingdom of God, people can't help but notice something different, something special about your marriage. They'll see your warmth and affection for one another and the confidence that comes from knowing you are loved, not only by each other, but by God.

Sometimes you'll forget this. Sometimes you'll think the success of your marriage depends entirely on you and your own will power or perceptions. Should this happen, you'll try to manage in your own strength and self-assurance, but you will eventually fail.

Without God, all is lost. With Him, nothing is. He has the power to preserve, protect, renew, revive, and uplift your marriage into His spirit, His kingdom. God loves you. He cares about you. If you happen to wander off, He knows how to draw you back into His embrace. He knows where to find you.

Do you know where to find—and keep on finding—Him? Throughout your married life, you will discover God in His word and your devotional times together. You will hear Him as you seek His insights and personal direction for you in daily times of prayer—prayers that speak and listen. You will recognize Him as you sense His ongoing healing of your body, mind, and spirit. You'll see His power as you forgive. You'll feel His presence as you praise Him and give Him the credit, the glory for your love and the blessings of your married life in Him.

Prayer: Dear Father in Heaven, let Your name always be holy in our hearts. Let Your kingdom come, Your will be done in us and in our marriage. Give us this day all that we need to be healed and to love and serve you well. Lead us not into the temptation of wanting our own wills, and deliver us from the evil of thwarted, twisted love. Forgive us our trespasses against You and each other, and help us to forgive those who bring us no comfort and give us no peace. Restore us, Lord. Let our marriage be a blessing to You and all those with whom we have contact. Help us to live, not in our own little world and ways, but in Your kingdom and Your power, bringing glory to You always in Jesus' name.

Journey with God: What's next? Ask God to direct you into a study of the Bible or biblical topics. For instance, see what His word says about marriage. Use a concordance to find scriptural references to related words such as *husband, wife, wed, love, family*. Ask God to remind you to pray for each other every day.

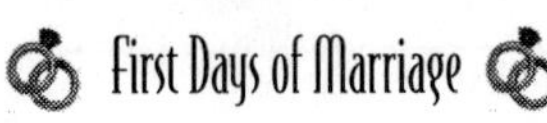